IF YOU want to initial this book when
read, please do so in one of the
squares below.

SCHOTT'S ORIGINAL
MISCELLANY

Conceived, written, and designed by

BEN SCHOTT

BLOOMSBURY

Schott's Original Miscellany™

Published by Bloomsbury Publishing Plc.
38 Soho Square, London, W1D 3HB, UK

www.miscellanies.info

10 9 8 7 6 5 4

Cover illustration © Alison Lang 2002

Illustrations on p.14 & p.87 are from *Open Here* (Thames & Hudson)
by kind permission of the authors, P. Mijksennar, & P. Westendorp.
Illustration on p.69 courtesy of the Royal National Institute for the Deaf.

ISBN 0-7475-6320-9

ISBN is the International Standard Book Number. It is always a ten digit code, and
whilst it is not essential for a published book to have an ISBN, the number is widely
used by booksellers, libraries, publishers, and distributors for cataloguing and stock
control. The ten digits are divided into four sections, separated by hyphens or spaces.
The first section identifies the national, geographical, or linguistic grouping of the
publisher; the second identifies the name of the publisher; the third identifies the title
or edition; and the fourth is a check-digit used to mathematically validate the ISBN.

A CIP catalogue record for this book is available from the British Library.

Designed and typeset by BEN SCHOTT
Printed in Great Britain by CLAYS Ltd., ST IVES Plc.

SCHOTT'S ORIGINAL
MISCELLANY

An encyclopaedia? A dictionary? An almanac? An anthology? A lexicon?
A treasury? A commonplace? An amphigouri? A vade-mecum?

Well… yes. *Schott's Original Miscellany* is all of these and, of course, more.

Schott's Original Miscellany is a snapper-up of unconsidered trifles. Its
purpose is to gather the flotsam and jetsam of the conversational tide.
Importantly, *Schott's Original Miscellany* makes very few claims to be
exhaustive, authoritative, or even practical. It does, however, claim to be
essential. It is, perhaps, possible to live one's life without *Schott's Original
Miscellany*, but it seems a curious and brave thing to attempt.

> MISCELLANY [mis.sel.iny] *noun* 1: A collection,
> medley, or mixture. 2: A collection of papers or
> treaties on a particular subject. 3: A volume or
> publication containing miscellaneous information
> of general interest on a variety of subjects. [OED]

―――――― TO FORGIVE, DIVINE ――――――

Painstaking efforts have been made to ensure that all of the information
contained within the *Miscellany* is correct. But, as Alexander Pope noted,
'to err is human'. Consequently, the author can accept no responsibility if
you play the wrong hand in poker; fly the Union Flag on an inappropriate
day; get lost on the way to John o'Groats; order the wrong sort of sushi;
shrink all of your socks; or say something utterly come-hither in Swedish.

Many of the facts within the book are the subject of debate and dispute.
A brief discussion of just a few such disputations can be found on p.153.

If you have suggestions[†], corrections, clarifications, or questions, please
email them to comments@miscellanies.info – or send them to the author
c/o Bloomsbury Publishing Plc., 38 Soho Square, London, W1D 3HB, UK.

―――――――――――――――――――――――――――――――――――――――

[†] The author reserves the right to treat any and all suggestions as his own, and to use them in
future editions, other related or unrelated projects, or just to add colour to his conversation.

THE FOLLOWING PEOPLE deserve their share of the blame:

Jonathan, Judith, and Geoffrey Schott.

Clare Algar, Louisa Allen, Stephen Aucutt, Joanna Begent,
Paul Binski, Martin Birchall, James Brabazon, John Casey,
James Coleman, Martin Colyer, Victoria Cook,
Aster Crawshaw, Rosemary Davidson, Jody Davies,
Jennifer Epworth, Penny Gillinson, Gaynor Hall,
Elinor Hodgson, Julian Hodgson, Miriam Hodgson,
Hugo de Klee, Alison Lang, Rachel Law, John Lloyd,
Jess Manson, Michael Manson, Susannah McFarlane,
Polly Napper, Cally Poplak, Daniel Rosenthal,
Tom Rosenthal, Ann Warnford-Davis, and William Webb.

To them my thanks are due for suggestions, advice, encouragement,
expert opinions, and other such things. If glaring errors exist within this
book, it's probably their fault.

'Let us not take it for granted that life exists

more fully in what is commonly thought big

than in what is commonly thought small.'

— VIRGINIA WOOLF

─────── GOLF STROKE NOMENCLATURE ───────

Double Bogey	+2	-1	Birdie
Bogey	+1	-2	Eagle
Par	0	-3	Albatross, Double Eagle

─────────────── HAT TAX ───────────────

Between 1784 and 1811, the British government levied a tax on the sale of hats. A graduated scale existed, ranging from 3*d* [on hats costing less than 4*s*], to 2*s* [for hats costing more than12*s*]. Purveyors of hats were obliged to purchase a Licence [£2 in London, 5*s* outside], and to display a sign proclaiming them a *Dealer in Hats by Retail*. To enforce this tax, duty-stamps were printed which had to be pasted into the lining of every hat. Evasion of the Hat Tax, by retailer or hat-wearer, was punishable by a fine; forgery of hat-duty stamps was ultimately punishable by death. For some curious reason, the tax applied only to men's hats. Similar taxes of the time included: Glove Tax (1785–94); Almanac Tax (1711–1834); Dice Duty (1711–1862); Hair-Powder Tax (1786–1869); Perfume Tax (1786–1800); and Wallpaper Tax (1712–1836). Perhaps the best-known duty of this type is Window Tax, levied first in 1697 to replace revenue lost through coin-clipping. Initially, nearly every house was charged 2*s*; properties with 10–20 windows paid 4*s*; and those with more than 20 windows paid 8*s*. These charges soon escalated, and consequently the practice of 'stopping up' became common. Windows were exempt from the count if they were permanently filled with materials matching the adjacent walls. Inspectors would regularly count exposed windows and ensure any stopped windows had not 'broken out'. Over time, the tax grew more unpopular since it became increasingly iniquitous, and it deprived residents (especially those in already disadvantaged areas) of daylight. In 1851 the tax was abolished.

─────── CHARACTERISTICS OF LIVING THINGS ───────

Movement · Respiration · Sensitivity · Growth · Reproduction
Excretion · Nutrition · [useful acronym: MRS GREN]

─────────────── SHOELACE LENGTH ───────────────

Pairs of holes	length (cm)		
2	45	5	75
3	45 *or* 60	6	90 *or* 110
4	60	8	150
		9	180

CRICKETING DISMISSALS

Hit Wicket · Caught · Bowled · Run Out · Handled Ball · Stumped
Hit Ball Twice · Timed Out · Leg Before Wicket · Obstructed Field

NOUNS OF ASSEMBLAGE

a malapertness of pedlars
a spring of teals
a gang of elk
a murmuration of starlings
a suit of sails
a wilderness of monkeys
a doping of sheldrake
a clutch of eggs
a coven of witches
a staff of servants
a field of runners
a sheaf of arrows
a chattering of choughs
a cete of badgers
a bench of bishops
a murder of crows
a bundle of rags
a barren of mules

a pontification of priests
a rag of colts
a walk of snipe
an exaltation of larks
a muster of peacocks
a desert of lapwing
a drift of swine
a stud of mares
a parliament of rooks & owls
a glozing of taverners
a covey of ptarmigan
a business of ferrets
a drunkship of cobblers
a sounder of wild boar
a nye of pheasants
a fall of woodcock
a sege of herons
a herd of curlews

BETTING ODDS SLANG

Evens	Levels, Scotch	7/1	Nevs
2/1	Bottle	8/1	T.H.
3/1	Carpet, Gimmel	9/1	Enin
4/1	Rouf	10/1	Cockle, Net
5/1	Hand	11/10	Tips
5/2	Face	33/1	Double Carpet
6/1	X's	100/30	Burlington Bertie

THE FLAG OF GUADELOUPE

The flag consists of horizontal bands which, from the top down, are:
narrow green, thin white stipe, wide red band, thin white stripe, and
narrow green. A five-pointed gold star is located in the middle of the red
band, on the hoist side. The flag of France is flown for official occasions.

─────────── PRESIDENTS OF THE USA ───────────

George Washington[§] .. 1789–1797[F]	Benjamin Harrison[B] .... 1889–1893[R]
John Adams[4,H] .... 1797–1801[F]	Grover Cleveland....... 1893–1897[D]
Thomas Jefferson[§,4] ... 1801–1809[DR]	William McKinley[†] .... 1897–1901[R]
James Madison ...... 1809–1817[DR]	Theodore Roosevelt[§,H,P] 1901–1909[R]
James Monroe[4] ...... 1817–1825[DR]	William Taft........ 1909–1913[R]
John Q. Adams[H] ...... 1825–1829[DR]	Woodrow Wilson[P,M] .... 1913–1921[D]
Andrew Jackson .... 1829–1837[D]	Warren Harding........ 1921–1923[R]
Martin Van Buren..... 1837–1841[D]	Calvin Coolidge........ 1923–1929[R]
William Harrison ..... 1841–1841[W]	Herbert Hoover[Q]....... 1929–1933[R]
John Tyler[M]............ 1841–1845[W]	Franklin Roosevelt[H] .... 1933–1945[D]
James Knox Polk ...... 1845–1849[D]	Harry S. Truman[L]...... 1945–1953[D]
Zachary Taylor .... 1849–1850[W]	Dwight Eisenhower .... 1953–1961[R]
Millard Fillmore....... 1850–1853[W]	John F. Kennedy[†,H,G] .. 1961–1963[D]
Franklin Pierce .... 1853–1857[D]	Lyndon Johnson........ 1963–1969[D]
James Buchanan[U]...... 1857–1861[D]	Richard Nixon[Q] .... 1969–1974[R]
Abraham Lincoln[§,†,B] .. 1861–1865[R]	Gerald Ford[L] .... 1974–1976[R]
Andrew Johnson....... 1865–1869[N]	James Carter .... 1976–1981[D]
Ulysses S. Grant[B]...... 1869–1877[R]	Ronald Reagan .... 1981–1988[R]
Rutherford Hayes[B,H] ... 1877–1881[R]	George Bush[G,L] .... 1988–1993[R]
James Garfield[†,B,L] ..... 1881–1881[R]	William Clinton[L]....... 1993–2001[D]
Chester Arthur .... 1881–1885[R]	George W. Bush[H] ...... 2001–[R]
Grover Cleveland[M] .... 1885–1889[D]	

Key: [F]ederal · [D]emocrat · [W]hig · [R]epublican · [N]on-partisan · Died on [4]th July
Was [B]earded · [§] carved on Mount Rushmore ·[U]nmarried · Attended [H]arvard
[G]emini · [Q]uaker · [P]eace Prize Winner · [M]arried in Office · [L]eft-handed
[†]Assassinated: LINCOLN *John Wilkes Booth* · GARFIELD *Charles J Guiteau*
McKINLEY *Leon Czolgosz* · KENNEDY *Lee Harvey Oswald*

─────────── NOTIFIABLE DISEASES ───────────

Doctors have a legal duty to report incidents of the following diseases:

Public Health (Control of Disease) Act 1984, s.10 & 11
Cholera · Plague · Relapsing fever · Smallpox · Typhus · Food poisoning
Public Health (Infectious Diseases) Regulations 1988 (S.I.1988 No.1546)
Acute encephalitis · Acute poliomyelitis · Anthrax · Diphtheria · Dysentery
Food poisoning · Leptospirosis · Malaria · Measles · Meningitis
Meningococcal septicaemia (without meningitis) · Mumps
Ophthalmia neonatorum · Paratyphoid fever · Rabies · Rubella
Scarlet fever · Tetanus · Tuberculosis · Typhoid fever · Viral haemorrhagic
fever · Viral hepatitis · Hepatitis A, B. & C · Whooping cough · Yellow fever

———————————————— JURY SERVICE ————————————————

Under the provisions of the Juries Act 1974, an individual is qualified to serve as a juror if they are registered as a parliamentary or local-government elector; are between the ages of 18 and 70; and have been ordinarily resident in the United Kingdom, Channel Islands, or Isle of Man for any period of at least five years since the age of 13. There are three reasons why an individual might not participate in jury-service:

INELIGIBLE

i The judiciary.
ii Those concerned with the administration of justice: e.g. barristers, solicitors, forensic scientists, prison governors, policemen.
iii The clergy: e.g. men in holy orders; regular ministers of any religious denomination; and vowed members of religious orders.
iv The mentally ill.

DISQUALIFIED

i Any person sentenced to more than five years in prison.
ii Any person who has served any part of a sentence of imprisonment during the previous ten years.
iii Any person who has been placed on probation during the last five years.
iv Any person on bail.

EXCUSED

i Persons over 65.
ii Members and officers of the Houses of Parliament.
iii European MPs.
iv Welsh Assembly members.
v Serving members of HM naval, air, or military forces.
vi Registered, practising doctors, dentists, nurses, midwives, vets, and pharmacists.
vii Those practising members of religious orders whose beliefs are incompatible with service.

In addition, a person may be excused from jury duty if they have previously served within two years of a summons.

Persons falling into one of the Excusable categories are not exempt from the obligation to serve until they are excused from attending.

———————————————— ALCOHOL MEASURES ————————————————

BEER		SPIRITS	
nip	¼ pint	tot [whisky]	⅙ ⅛, ¼, or ⅓ gill
small	½ pint	noggin	1 gill
large	1 pint	bottle	1⅙ pints
flagon	1 quart	GILL	
anker	10 gallons	1 gill	¼ pint
tun	216 gallons	modern measures	25ml & 35ml

---------- SCOVILLE SCALE ----------

In 1912 Wilbur Scoville developed his now famous method to chart the comparative heat of different chillis (*J. Am. Pharm. Assoc.* 1912; 1:453–4). The greater number of Scoville Units, the hotter the chilli. For example:

Bell Pepper. . . . . 0 *Scoville Units (SU)*
Peperocini, Cherry Pepper 100–500
New Mexico, Aji Panca 500–1,000
Ancho, Passila, Espanola 1,000–1,500
Sandia, Rocotillo, Cascabel, Poblano 1,500–2,500
Jalapeno, Mirasol. 2,500–5,000
Chilcostle, Louisiana Hot. 5,000–10,000
de Arbol, Serrano, Japones 10,000–30,000
Piquin, Aji, Cayenne, Tabasco. 30,000–50,000
Chiltepin, Tepin. 50,000–80,000
Habanero, Scotch Bonnet. 80,000–300,000
Pure Capsaicin. 16,000,000

This can only be a rough guide, since the heat of chillis can vary from pepper to pepper.

---------- HOW TO TIE A BOW-TIE ----------

---------- A CERTAIN CHINESE ENCYCLOPAEDIA ----------

Although possibly an elaborate literary joke, one of the most curious lists is that quoted (and perhaps invented) by J.L. Borges. In one of his essays (made famous by Michel Foucault), Borges claims that Dr Franz Kuhn discovered a 'certain Chinese encyclopaedia' entitled *Celestial Empire of Benevolent Knowledge,* which stated that all animals can be classified thus:

[a] belonging to the Emperor · [b] embalmed · [c] tame
[d] sucking pigs · [e] sirens · [f] fabulous · [g] stray dogs
[h] included in the present classification · [i] that shake like a fool
[j] innumerable · [k] drawn with a very fine camel-hair brush
[l] etcetera · [m] having just broken the water pitcher
[n] that, if seen from a distance, look like flies.

LAND'S END TO JOHN O'GROATS

Land's End · Join the A30 at Trevescan · Continue on the A30 past Penzance · Join the M5 at junction 31 south of Exeter · Join the M6 at W. Bromwich towards Stafford and Stoke on Trent · Leave the M6 at junction 44 Carlisle north, and join the A74 · Join the A74(M) at junction 22 near Gretna · The A74(M) becomes the M74 at junction 13 near Abington · Continue on the M74 until junction 4 · Join the M73 north · At junction 3 of the M73, join the A80 east towards Cumbernauld and Falkirk · Leave the A80 at junction 4, and join the M80 north · Leave the M80 and join the M9 towards Perth · At junction 11 join the A9 and continue north · Turn onto the A99 at Latherton · Continue past Wick, Keiss, and the Stacks of Duncansby · *John o'Groats*

MILEAGE – *c*.835 miles · DRIVING TIME – *c*.16 hours

THAMES CROSSINGS

Kew · Chiswick · Barnes · Hammersmith · Putney · Wandsworth · Battersea · Albert · Chelsea · Vauxhall · Lambeth · Westminster · Hungerford Foot · Waterloo · Blackfriars · Millennium · Southwark · London · Tower · Rotherhithe Tunnel · Greenwich Foot Tunnel · Blackwall Tunnel

SOME BINGO CALLS

Man Alive	5	Red Raw	64
Doctor's Orders	9	Clickety Click	66
Legs Eleven	11	Bang on the Drum	71
Thee and Me	23	Trombones	76
Dirty Gertie	30	One More Time	79
More than Eleven	37	Stop and Run	81
Halfway There	45	Between the Sticks	86
Tweak of the Thumb	51	Two Fat Ladies	88
Brighton Line	59	Top of the Shop	90

THE CINQUE PORTS

Sandwich · Dover · Hythe · Romney · Hastings
[plus the two 'Antient Towns' of Rye and Winchelsea]

COUNTING FRUIT STONES

When shall I marry?
This year, next year, sometime, never.
What will my husband be?
Tinker, tailor, soldier, sailor, rich-man, poor-man, beggar-man, thief.
What shall I wear?
Silk, satin, cotton, rags.
How shall I get it?
Given, borrowed, bought, stolen.
How shall I get to church?
Coach, carriage, wheelbarrow, cart.
Where shall I live?
Big house, little house, pig-sty, barn.

SOME FAMOUS HORSES

LAMRI	King Arthur	VIC	Lt.-Col. Custer
BLACKIE	Chief Sitting Bull	KANTAKA	Buddha
MAGNOLIA	George Washington	FUBUKI	Emperor Hirohito
STRYMON	Xerxes	SILVER	The Lone Ranger
BLACK BESS	Dick Turpin	HAIZUM	Archangel Gabriel
ROSINANTE	Don Quixote	COPENHAGEN	Wellington
ARION	Hercules	SHADOWFAX	Gandalf
MARENGO[†]	Napoleon	BUCEPHALUS	Alexander the Great
HIPPOCAMPUS	Neptune	TRIGGER	Roy Rogers

[†]*Marengo was captured by the British. She outlived Napoleon by eight years, and her skeleton is preserved at London's National Army Museum. A snuff-box was made from one of her hoofs.*

BIKINI & DEFCON

The term BIKINI is employed by British armed forces around the world to indicate the level of terrorist threat. The BIKINI ALERT STATES are:

WHITE · BLACK · BLACK SPECIAL · AMBER · RED

Each level indicates a greater degree of threat. BIKINI states are usually set at a local level, indicating the perceived risk at specific locations. The US Government operates a series of 'progressive alert postures' indicating the overall level of combat readiness: DEFence CONditions. These are part of a wider schemata of ALERTCONs and EMERGCONs. The DEFCON status is from 5 (normal peacetime readiness) to 1 (maximum force readiness) and whilst the DEFCON level is classified, some state that at the height of the 1962 Cuban Missile Crisis, the US military advanced to DEFCON 2.

SUMÓ

Bouts of *sumó* take place in the *dohyó* (ring) and are governed by the *gyóji* (referee) and five other judges. As befits a Japanese martial art, the ritual and courtesy of *sumó* are axiomatic. Wrestlers must be naked except for a *mawashi* (loincloth), 40cm wide, which is tied round the body in a series of precise moves. Each bout starts with complex standing, pledging, and purification movements, until the act of *tachiai* commences and the combatants rise to fight. A competitor loses the bout when any part of his body other than the soles of his feet touches the floor; when he is pushed from the boundary of the *dohyó*; or when he has performed *kinjite* (an illegal move). Illegal moves include slapping from the side, kicking, biting, and grabbing. In an attempt to qualify for recognition as an official Olympic sport, Sumó is adopting the following weight categories:

[♂] <85kg	LIGHT	<65kg [♀]
[♂] <115kg	MIDDLE	<80kg [♀]
[♂] >115kg	HEAVY	>80kg [♀]
[♂] unlimited	OPEN	unlimited [♀]

CURIOUS SURNAME PRONUNCIATIONS

as written	as pronounced
Althorp	Althrup, Altrup, Atrup
Auchinlech	Af-lek
Beauchamp	Beacham
Beaulieu	Bewley
Belvoir	Beaver
Blount	Blunt
Blyth	Bly
Bohun	Boon
Caius	Keeys
Cherwell	Charwell
Cholmondley	Chumley
Cockburn	Coburn
Colquhoun	Cahoon
Crespigny	Crepiny
De la Warr	Della-ware
Devereux	Dever-uks
Featherstonehaugh	Fanshaw
Fiennes	Fines
Glamis	Glarms
Harewood	Harwood
Home	Hume
Houghton	Horton, Howton
Keynes	Kaynz
Knollys	Nowls
Le Fanu	Leff-new
Legh	Lee
Magdalene	Maudlin
Mainwaring	Mannering
Marjoribanks	Marchbanks
Menzies	Ming-is
Poulett	Pawlet
Ruthven	Riven
Sandys	Sandz
St Clair	Sinclair
St John	Sin-jen
Theobald	Tibbald
Tyrwhitt	Tirit
Waldegrave	Wawgrave
Wavertree	Wawtry
Wemyss	Wemz, Weemz
Woolfhardisworthy	Woolsey
Worcester	Woo-ster
Wymondham	Wind-am

———————————— PLIMSOLL LINE ————————————

The Plimsoll Line was named after the English politician Samuel Plimsoll (1824–98), who successfully campaigned for the official establishment of safe loading-limits for shipping. This put an end to the insurance fraud sometimes practised, whereby overladen 'coffin-ships' were put to sea in the hope that they would sink, thereby justifying a claim. A series of modern Load Lines has been established through international agreement, and the following abbreviations are painted onto each ship:

TF	Tropical Fresh Water	
F	Fresh Water	
T	Tropical Sea Water	
S	Summer Sea Water	
W	Winter Sea Water	
WNA	Winter North Atlantic	

[Different schemata exist for Timber Load Lines, vessels sailing on the Great American Lakes, and so on.]

———— LINES OF THE LONDON UNDERGROUND ————

Line	Length	Opened c.	Busiest Station	Colour	Stations
Bakerloo	23.2 *km*	1906	Oxford Circus	brown	25
Central	74	1900	Oxford Circus	red	49
Circle	22.5	1863–5	Victoria	yellow	27
District	64	1868	Victoria	green	60
East London	8	1843–63	Canada Water	orange	9
Hammersmith	26.5	1863–4	King's Cross	pink	28
Jubilee[†]	36.2	1880	Bond Street	silver	27
Metropolitan	66.7	1868	Baker Street	maroon	34
Northern	58	1890	Leicester Square	black	51
Piccadilly	71	1906	Piccadilly Circus	navy blue	52
Victoria	21	1968	Victoria	light blue	16
Waterloo & City	2.4	1898	—	cyan	2

[†] *The Jubilee Line is the only line which interconnects with every other line.*

———— THE FIVE REGULAR PLATONIC SOLIDS ————

Regular polyhedron	*Faces*		
tetrahedron............4 triangles		octahedron.............8 triangles	
cube.....................6 squares		dodecahedron.......12 pentagons	
		icosahedron...........20 triangles	

THE BOND FILMS

FILM TITLE	007	YEAR	VILLAIN	BOND GIRL	KEY CAR
Dr No	SC	62	Doctor No	Ursula Andress · *Honey Ryder*	Sunbeam Alpine
From Russia With Love	SC	63	Red Grant	Daniela Bianchi · *Tatiana Romanova*	Bentley Mark IV
Goldfinger	SC	64	Goldfinger	Honor Blackman · *Pussy Galore*	Aston Martin DB5
Thunderball	SC	65	Emilio Largo	Claudine Auger · *Domino*	Aston Martin DB5
You Only Live Twice	SC	67	Blofeld	Akiko Wakabayashi · *Aki*	Toyota 2000 GT
On Her Majesty's Secret Service	GL	69	Blofeld	Diana Rigg · *Tracy Vicenzo*	Aston Martin DB5
Diamonds Are Forever	SC	71	Blofeld	Jill St John · *Tiffany Case*	Moon Buggy
Live And Let Die	RM	73	Dr Kananga	Jane Seymour · *Solitaire*	Double Decker
The Man With The Golden Gun	RM	74	Scaramanga	Britt Ekland · *Mary Goodnight*	AMC Hornet
The Spy Who Loved Me	RM	77	Karl Stromberg	Barbara Bach · *Anya Amasova*	Lotus Esprit
Moonraker	RM	79	Hugo Drax	Lois Chiles · *Dr Holly Goodhead*	Gondola
For Your Eyes Only	RM	81	Kristatos	Caroline Bouquet · *Melina Havelock*	Citroën 2CV
Octopussy	RM	83	Kamal Khan	Maud Adams · *Octopussy*	Mercedes 250SE
A View To A Kill	RM	85	Max Zorin	Tanya Roberts · *Stacey Sutton*	Renault 11
The Living Daylights	TD	87	Koskov	Maryam D'Abo · *Kara Milovy*	Aston Martin Volante
Licence To Kill	TD	89	Franz Sanchez	Carey Lowell · *Pam Bouvier*	Kenworth Tanker
GoldenEye	PB	95	Alec Trevelyan	Izabell Scorupco · *Natalya Simonova*	BMW Z3
Tomorrow Never Dies	PB	97	Elliott Carver	Michelle Yeoh · *Wai Lin*	BMW 750iL
The World Is Not Enough	PB	99	Renard	Denise Richards · *Christmas Jones*	BMW Z8
Die Another Day	PB	02	Zao	Halle Berry · *Jinx*	Aston Martin V12 Vanquish

[007s: SC – Sean Connery · GL – George Lazenby · RM – Roger Moore · TD – Timothy Dalton · PB – Pierce Brosnan]

COCKNEY RHYMING SLANG

Adam and Eve	Believe
Alan Wickers	Knickers
Almond Rocks	Socks
Apples and Pears	Stairs
Aristotle	Bottle
Artful Dodger	Lodger
Ascot Races	Braces
Baked Bean	Queen
Baker's Dozen	Cousin
Ball and Chalk	Walk
Barnaby Rudge	Judge
Barnet Fair	Hair
Basil Fawlty	Balti
Battlecruiser	Boozer
Boat Race	Face
Bob Hope	Soap
Boracic Lint	Skint
Brahms and Liszt	Pissed
Brass Tacks	Facts
Bread and Honey	Money
Bricks and Mortar	Daughter
Bristol City	Titty
Brown Bread	Dead
Bubble and Squeak	Greek
Butcher's Hook	Look
Chalfont St Giles	Piles
Chalk Farm	Arm
China Plate	Mate
Cobbler's Awls	Balls
Cock and Hen	Ten
Currant Bun	Sun
Daisy Roots	Boots
Darby and Joan	Moan
Dicky Bird	Word
Dicky Dirt	Shirt
Dinky Doos	Shoes
Dog and Bone	Phone
Duck and Dive	Skive
Duke of Kent	Rent
Dustbin Lid	Kid
Flowery Dell	Cell
Frog and Toad	Road
Gregory Peck	Cheque
George Raft	Draft
Gypsy's Kiss	Piss
Hampton Wick	Prick
Hank Marvin	Starving
Jam Jar	Car
Jimmy Riddle	Piddle
Aunt Joanna	Piano
Khyber Pass	Arse
Kick and Prance	Dance
Lady Godiva	Fiver
Lionel Blairs	Flares
Loaf of Bread	Head
Mickey Bliss	Piss
Mince Pies	Eyes
Mork and Mindy	Windy
Mutt and Jeff	Deaf
North and South	Mouth
Oily Rag	Fag
Peckham Rye	Tie
Pen and Ink	Stink
Plates of Meat	Feet
Pony and Trap	Crap
Porky Pies	Lies
Richard the 3rd	Turd
Rosie Lee	Tea
Round the Houses	Trousers
Rub-a-Dub	Pub
Ruby Murray	Curry
Salmon and Trout	Snout
Sherbet Dab	Cab
Skin and Blister	Sister
Sky Rocket	Pocket
Sweeny Todd	Flying Squad
Syrup of Figs	Wig
Tea Leaf	Thief
Tit for Tat (Titfer)	Hat
Todd Sloane	Alone
Tom and Dick	Sick
Tom-foolery	Jewellery
Tommy Trinder	Window
Trouble and Strife	Wife
Vera Lynn	Gin
Whistle and Flute	Suit

────── ORDERS TO FIRE CANNON ──────

Firing a single shot from a stowed and loaded cannon in Nelson's navy was regulated by the following sequence of orders:

Silence!
Cast loose your gun!
Level your gun!
Take out your tampion!
Prime!
Run out your gun!
Point your gun!
Fire!
Worm and sponge!
Load with cartridge!
Load with shot and wad to your shot!
Ram home shot and wad!
Put in your tampion!
House your gun!
Secure your gun!

────── COTTON MEASURES ──────

1 thread	54 inches	1 hank	7 skeins
1 skein	80 threads	1 spindle	18 hanks

PUBLICATIONS TO BE CARRIED
BY UNITED KINGDOM SHIPS

*Publications which must be carried by sea-going passenger vessels
and all other vessels over 300 gross tons:*
IMO International Code of Signals · The Mariner's Handbook

*Publications for which only those parts relevant to a vessel's voyage
and operation must be carried:*
Merchant Shipping Notices, Marine Guidance Notes and Marine
Information Notes · Notices to Mariners · IMO Lists of Radio Signals
IMO Lists of Lights · IMO Sailing Directions · Nautical Almanac
Navigational Tables · Tide Tables · Tidal Stream Atlases
Operating and maintenance instructions for navigational aids carried

[Nautical publications must be the latest editions and must incorporate
the latest relevant supplements and updates.]

DR JOHNSON

One of the towering literary figures of his age, Samuel Johnson (1709–84) was a lexicographer, dramatist, novelist, critic, poet, editor, and conversationalist. Johnson's verbal dexterity (immortalised in great part by his companion and biographer James Boswell) demonstrates a masterful command of English, and shows his unique insight into human nature.

WORK & MONEY

No man but a blockhead ever wrote, except for money.

Faults and defects every work of man must have.

Whatever you have, spend less.

What we hope ever to do with ease, we must learn first to do with diligence.

As peace is the end of war, so to be idle is the ultimate purpose of the busy.

Those who attain to any excellence commonly spend life in some single pursuit, for excellence is not often gained upon easier terms.

It is wonderful when a calculation is made, how little the mind is actually employed in the discharge of any profession.

All intellectual improvement arises from leisure.

The true art of memory is the art of attention.

LANGUAGE

In all pointed sentences, some degree of accuracy must be sacrificed to conciseness.

Example is always more efficacious than precept.

Read over your compositions, and where ever you meet with a passage which you think is particularly fine, strike it out.

Every quotation contributes something to the stability or enlargement of the language.

Dictionaries are like watches, the worst is better than none, and the best cannot be expected to go quite true.

The end of writing is to instruct; the end of poetry is to instruct by pleasing.

FOOD & DRINK

Claret is the liquor for boys; port for men; but he who aspires to be a hero ... must drink brandy.

A cucumber should be well sliced, and dressed with pepper and vinegar, and then thrown out, as good for nothing.

SHAKESPEARE

[Shakespeare] sacrifices virtue to convenience, and is so much more careful to please than to instruct, that he seems to write without any moral purpose.

———— DR JOHNSON cont. ————

FRIENDSHIP

If a man does not make new acquaintance as he advances through life, he will soon find himself alone. A man should keep his friendship in constant repair.

Always, Sir, set a high value on spontaneous kindness.

To let friendship die away by negligence and silence is certainly not wise. It is voluntarily to throw away one of the greatest comforts of the weary pilgrimage.

Distance has the same effect on the mind as on the eye.

The longer we live the more we think and the higher the value we put on friendship and tenderness towards parents and friends.

How few of his friends' houses would a man choose to be at when he is ill.

HUMAN NATURE

Almost every man wastes part of his life attempting to display qualities which he doesn't possess.

Nothing can please many, and please long, but just representations of general nature.

Nothing is more hopeless than a scheme of merriment.

Whoever thinks of going to bed before twelve o'clock is a scoundrel.

It is wonderful that five thousand years have now elapsed since the creation of the world, and still it is undecided whether or not there has ever been an instance of the spirit of any person appearing after death. All argument is against it; but all belief is for it.

All envy would be extinguished, if it were universally known that there are none to be envied.

We are all prompted by the same motives, all deceived by the same fallacies, all animated by hope, obstructed by danger, entangled by desire, and seduced by pleasure.

It matters not how a man dies, but how he lives. The act of dying is not of importance, it lasts so short a time.

He was dull in a new way, and that made many people think him great.

LONDON

Sir, if you wish to have a just notion of the magnitude of this city, you must not be satisfied with seeing its great streets and squares, but must survey the innumerable little lanes and courts. It is not in the showy evolutions of buildings, but in the multiplicity of human habitations which are crowded together, that the wonderful immensity of London consists.

When a man is tired of London, he is tired of life; for there is in London all that life can afford.

—— COUNTRIES WITH COMPULSORY VOTING ——

Argentina · Australia · Austria · Belgium · Bolivia · Brazil · Chile
Congo · Costa Rica · Cyprus · Dominican Rep. · Ecuador · Egypt
El Salvador · Fiji · Greece · Honduras · Lebanon · Libya · Liechtenstein
Luxembourg · Madagascar · Mexico · Nauru · Panama · Paraguay
Philippines · Singapore · Thailand · Turkey · Uruguay · Venezuela

—— HAZCHEM WARNING PLATES ——

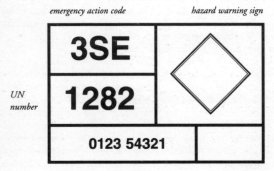

emergency action code   *hazard warning sign*

UN number

0123 54321

specialist advice phone number   *company logo*

The three-character EMERGENCY ACTION CODE gives the emergency-services information on how to deal with an incident involving hazardous material. The initial number identifies the method of fire-fighting; the second letter indicates the necessary safety precautions; and the presence of a final 'E' informs the emergency services of a hazard to public-safety.

1: Course Spray	2: Fine Spray	3: Foam	4: Dry Agent

P R	V	Chemical Suits	Dilute Spillage
S T	V	Breathing Apparatus	
W X	V	Chemical Suits	Contain Spillage
Y Z	V	Breathing Apparatus	
E	PUBLIC SAFETY HAZARD		
V	can be violently or explosively reactive		

—— SOME US CONSTITUTION AMENDMENTS ——

1st .... Freedom of religion, speech, press, assembly, and petition
2nd .... The right to bear arms
5th ...... Prevention of double-jeopardy; right against self-incrimination
8th .... Prevention of cruel or unusual punishments
13th .... Abolished slavery
15th ...... Right to vote regardless of race, colour, or previous servitude
16th .... Right of Congress to levy income taxes
19th .... Right of women to vote
21st .... Repeal of prohibition (18th Amendment)
22nd .... Limiting Presidents to two terms
26th .... Voting age of 18
27th .... Postponing Representatives' pay rises until new elections

—— BLOOD GROUP COMPATIBILITY ——

Recipient	Plasma	Whole Blood	Red Cells
O+	any O; A, B or AB	O+, O	O+, O-
O-	any O; A B or AB	O-	O-
A+	any A or AB	any A+, A-	any A+; A-; O+, O-
A-	any A or AB	A-	any A- or O-
B+	any B or AB	any B+ or B-	any B+; B-; O+ or O-
B-	any B or AB	B-	any B- or O-
AB+	any AB	any AB+ or AB-	any AB+; AB- A+, A-, B+, B-, O+, O-
AB-	AB	AB-	any AB-; A- B-, or O-

The above table should not be used as a guide, since many anomalies exist and un-crossmatched transfusions can cause life-threatening reactions.

MURDERS

term	killing of a
homicide	person
genocide	ethnic /national group
suicide	self
parenticide	parent
patricide	father
matricide	mother
fratricide	brother
sororicide	sister
mariticide	spouse
infanticide	infant
uxoricide	wife
parricide	kinsman
regicide	king
tyrannicide	tyrant
vaticide	prophet

CLASSICAL COLUMN TYPES

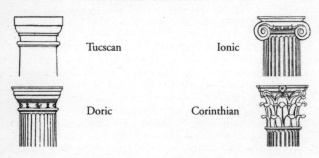

Tucscan

Ionic

Doric

Corinthian

PRECEDENCE OF THE GREAT 12 CITY LIVERY COMPANIES

1	Mercers
2	Grocers
3	Drapers
4	Fishmongers
5	Goldsmiths
6	Merchant Taylors†
7	Skinners†
8	Haberdashers
9	Salters
10	Ironmongers
11	Vintners
12	Clothworkers

[†Dispute between Merchant Taylors & Skinners as to which has precedence is thought to be the source of the expression 'at sixes and sevens'. By order of Alderman Billesden in 1484, the companies alternate in precedence yearly.]

CAVIAR

Caviar derives from the Turkish term for fish-eggs: *khavia*. Traditionally, 3 sturgeon species are fished for caviar: BELUGA, OSIETRA, & SEVRUGA.

─────────────── LONDON CLUBS ───────────────

foundation	club	membership
1693	White's, 37 St James's Street, SW1	♂
1762	Boodle's, 28 St James's Street, SW1	♂
1764	Brooks's, St James's Street, SW1	♂
1775	The Royal Thames Yacht Club, 60 Knightsbridge, SW1	☿
1819	Travellers' Club, 106 Pall Mall, SW1	♂
1824	The Oriental Club, Stratford Place, W1	{☿}
1824	The Athenæum, 107 Pall Mall, SW1	☿
1831	The Garrick Club, 15 Garrick Street, WC2	♂
1832	The City of London Club, 19 Old Broad Street, EC2	♂
1832	The Carlton Club, 69 St James's Street, SW1	{☿}
1836	The Reform Club, 104 Pall Mall, SW1	☿
1837	The Army and Navy Club, 36 Pall Mall, SW1	☿
1841	Pratt's Club, 14 Park Place, SW1	♂
1849	The East India Club, 16 St James's Square, SW1	♂
1857	The Savage Club, 9 Whitehall Place, W1	♂
1862	The Naval and Military Club, 4 St James's Square, W1	☿
1863	The Arts Club, 40 Dover Street, W1	☿
1868	The Turf Club, 5 Carlton House Terrace, SW1	{☿}
1868	The Savile Club, 69 Brook Street, W1	♂
1870	St Stephen's Club, 34 Queen Anne's Gate, SW1	☿
1876	The Beefsteak, 9 Irving Street, WC2	♂
1882	The National Liberal Club, 1 Whitehall Place, SW1	☿
1886	University Women's Club, 2 Audley Square, W1	♀
1891	The Caledonian Club, 9 Halkin Street, SW1	{☿}
1893	The Cavalry & Guards' Club, 127 Piccadilly, W1	{☿}
1895	The City University Club, 50 Cornhill, EC1	☿
1897	The RAC Club, 89 Pall Mall, SW1	☿
1908	The Wig & Pen Club, 229–230 Strand, WC2	☿
1910	The Royal Over-seas League, St James's Street, SW1	♀
1914	The City Livery Club, Victoria Embankment, EC4	☿
1918	The RAF Club, 128 Piccadilly, W1	☿
1919	Buck's, 18 Clifford Street, W1	♂
1935	The Lansdowne Club, 9 Fitzmaurice Place, W1	☿
1972	United Oxford & Cambridge Club, 71 Pall Mall, SW1	☿

Membership key: ♂ men only · ♀ women only · ☿ equal membership
{☿} men full membership, women associate membership.

─────────────── MARTINI ───────────────

⅓ Vermouth · ⅔ Dry Gin · *Shake, garnish, serve on or off the rocks.*

UNTIMELY POPSTAR DEATHS

POP-STAR	drugs 'n' alcohol	murder	traffic accident	plane crash	suicide	misadventure	CAUSE OF DEATH	AGED
Chet Baker						■	*death by defenestration*	58
Mark Bolan			■				*overdose of tree whilst driving*	29
John Bonham	■						*Led Zeppelin; vodka overdose*	32
Sonny Bono						■	*skied into a tree in Tahoe*	62
Jeff Buckley						■	*drowned in Mississippi River*	30
Tim Buckley	■						*mistook heroin for cocaine*	28
Karen Carpenter						■	*rock'n'roll underdose: anorexia*	32
Steve Clark	■						*Def Leppard; drink and drugs*	30
Kurt Cobain					■		*Nirvana; suicide (or murder?)*	27
Eddie Cochrane			■				*car crash on his way to airport*	21
Sam Cooke		■					*shot dead by a motel owner*	33
King Curtis		■					*murdered outside his own home*	37
'Mama' Cass						■	*ham sandwich asphyxiation*	32
Jerry Garcia	■						*Gratefully Dead via heroin*	53
Marvin Gaye		■					*shot dead by his father*	44
Lowell George	■						*Little Feat; big drug overdose*	34
Jimi Hendrix	■						*Drug overdose (suicide?)*	27
Buddy Holly				■			*killed in 'that' plane crash*	22
M. Hutchence					■		*suicide in his hotel room*	37
Brian Jones						■	*drowned in his swimming pool*	27
Janis Joplin	■						*accidental heroin overdose*	27
Paul Kossoff	■						*drug induced heart-attack*	25
John Lennon		■					*murdered by Mark Chapman*	40
Kirsty MacColl						■	*tragic jet-ski collision*	41
Joe Meek					■		*shot his landlady, and himself*	37
Keith Moon	■						*drink, drugs, and general excess*	31
Jim Morrison	■						*drink and possibly heroin too*	27
'Notorious' B.I.G.		■					*capped in a gangster-rap war*	24
Elvis Presley	■						*prescription drug-abuse*	42
Otis Redding				■			*killed in plane crash*	26
J.P. Richardson				■			*killed in 'that' plane crash*	28
Tupac Shakur		■					*capped in a gangster-rap war*	25
Vivian Stanshall						■	*Bonzo Dog Band; died in fire*	51
Richie Valens				■			*killed in 'that' plane crash*	17
Stevie Ray Vaughan				■			*helicopter flew into mountain*	35
Sid Vicious	■						*Sex Pistols; heroin overdose*	21
Gene Vincent	■						*general rock'n'roll excess*	36
Dennis Wilson						■	*drowned: Beach Boy not Buoy*	39

—————————— CAT'S EYE COLOURS ——————————

WHITE *separate lanes* · AMBER *mark offside of motorway*
RED *mark nearside of motorway* · BLUE *mark police-only slip roads*
GREEN *mark exit or entrance slip roads*
[Cat's Eyes were invented in 1933 by Percy Shaw, who in 1965 was awarded the OBE.]

—————————— MI5, &c ——————————

The various British Military Intelligence units are the subject of much
speculation, and only relatively recently have any MI departments been
officially acknowledged. Some departments were only temporary, many
have merged, others may be entirely apocryphal. A tentative list might be:

MI 1	Director of Military Intelligence; also cryptography
MI 2	Responsible for Russia and Scandinavia
MI 3	Responsible for Germany & Eastern Europe
MI 4	Aerial Reconnaissance during WWII
MI 5	Domestic intelligence and security
MI 6	Foreign intelligence and security
MI 8	Interception & interpretation of communications
MI 9	Clandestine operations · Escape and Evasion
MI 10	Weapons and technical analysis
MI 11	Field Security Police
MI 14	German specialists
MI 17	Secretariat body for MI departments
MI 19	POW debriefing unit

—————————— SANDRINGHAM TIME ——————————

King Edward VII introduced the custom of setting the 180 or so clocks
on the Sandringham Estate half an hour early to allow him more time to
shoot. As a consequence, all business when the King was at Sandringham
took place in this unique royal time zone. George V maintained this
tradition, but Edward VIII, when he acceded to the throne in 1936, reset
Sandringham's time-pieces in synchronicity with the rest of his kingdom.

—————————— BLOODY MARY ——————————

2 vodka · 3 tomato juice · ½ lemon juice · Ground salt & pepper
6 dashes Worcestershire sauce · 5 drops Tabasco · lemon & celery
Shake all the ingredients, add garnishes, and serve over crushed ice.

---------------- BALLISTIC MISSILE RANGES ----------------

SRBM....... Short Range Ballistic Missile .... <1,100 km
MRBM...... Medium Range Ballistic Missile .... 1,100–2,750 km
IRBM ...... Intermediate Range Ballistic Missile....... 2,750–5,500 km
ICBM .... Intercontinental Ballistic Missile .... >5,500 km

---------------- POLARI ----------------

Polari is the theatrical and homosexual slang prevalent in London during the 1950s and 60s. An eclectic mix of Italian, Romany, back-slang, Yiddish, naval slang, and theatre-speak, Polari first entered the public domain through BBC radio's *Round The Horn*. Here, Kenneth Williams and Hugh Paddick, playing the theatrical Julian and Sandy, 'scandalised' and delighted the British public every week with louche, camp innuendo.

balonie	rubbish	lilly (law)	police
bijou	small	mangarie	food
blag	pick up	mince	walk (effeminately)
bona	good	nanty	not, no, none
bona nochi	good night	naff	dull; straight
buvare	a drink	ogle	look, admire
cackle	talk, gossip	omi	man
charper	to search	omi-palone	homosexual
clobber	clothes	palone	woman
dinarly	money	riah	hair
dish	arse	scarper	to run off
dolly	pleasant	shush bag	hold-all
dona	woman	slap	makeup
drag	clothes	todd (Sloane)	alone
eek	face	trolling	to mince, walk
fantabulosa	excellent	vada	see, look at
lallies	legs	vogue	cigarette
lattie	house	yews	eyes

'vada that bona omi with his dolly eek and fantabulosa riah'

---------------- THIRTY DAYS ----------------

Thirty days hath September, April, June, and November;
All the rest have thirty-one, Excepting February alone,
Which hath but twenty-eight days clear,
And twenty-nine in each leap year.

THE BOAT RACE

1829 ..... O	1881 ..... O	⋮	1923 ..... O	1966 ..... O
1836 C	1882 ..... O	*Putney Bridge*	1924 C	1967 ..... O
1839 C	1883 ..... O	⋮	1925 C	1968 C
1840 C	1884 C	START	1926 C	1969 C
1841 C	1885 ..... O	⋮	1927 C	1970 C
1842 ..... O	1886 C	⋮	1928 C	1971 C
1845 C	1887 C	⋮	1929 C	1972 C
1846 C	1888 C	⋮	1930 C	1973 C
1849 C	1889 C	⋮	1931 C	1974 ..... O
1849 ..... O	1890 ..... O	1 MILE	1932 C	1975 C
1852 ..... O	1891 ..... O	⋮	1933 C	1976 ..... O
1854 ..... O	1892 ..... O	⋮	1934 C	1977 ..... O
1856 C	1893 ..... O	*Hammersmith Bridge*	1935 C	1978 ..... O
1857 ..... O	1894 ..... O		1936 C	1979 ..... O
1858 C	1895 ..... O	⋮	1937 ..... O	1980 ..... O
1859 ..... O	1896 ..... O	⋮	1938 ..... O	1981 ..... O
1860 C	1897 ..... O	⋮	1939 C	1982 ..... O
1861 ..... O	1898 ..... O	2 MILES	1946 ..... O	1983 ..... O
1862 ..... O	1899 C	⋮	1947 C	1984 ..... O
1863 ..... O	1900 C	⋮	1948 C	1985 ..... O
1864 ..... O	1901 ..... O	⋮	1949 C	1986 C
1865 ..... O	1902 C	⋮	1950 C	1987 ..... O
1866 ..... O	1903 C	⋮	1951 C	1988 ..... O
1867 ..... O	1904 C	3 MILES	1952 ..... O	1989 ..... O
1868 ..... O	1905 ..... O	⋮	1953 C	1990 ..... O
1869 ..... O	1906 C	*Barnes Bridge*	1954 ..... O	1991 ..... O
1870 C	1907 C		1955 C	1992 ..... O
1871 C	1908 C	⋮	1956 C	1993 C
1872 C	1909 ..... O	⋮	1957 C	1994 C
1873 C	1910 ..... O	⋮	1958 C	1995 C
1874 C	1911 ..... O	4 MILES	1959 ..... O	1996 C
1875 ..... O	1912 ..... O	⋮	1960 ..... O	1997 C
1876 C	1913 ..... O	— FINISH — 4 miles 374 yds	1961 C	1998 C
1877 ..... H	1914 C	⋮	1962 C	1999 C
1878 ..... O	1920 C	*Chiswick Bridge*	1963 ..... O	2000 ..... O
1879 C	1921 C		1964 C	2001 C
1880 ..... O	1922 C	⋮	1965 ..... O	2002 ..... O

Oxford Win [70] · *Cambridge Win [77]* · *Dead Heat [1]*

The Boat Race was started by two friends, Charles Merivale (Cambridge), and Charles [nephew of William] Wordsworth (Oxford). On 12 March 1829, Cambridge challenged Oxford – and the Boat Race was born. By tradition, the loser challenges the previous year's winner to the next race.

——— ENGLISH COIN SPECIFICATION ———

£2 Edge Inscription *Standing on the Shoulders of Giants* · *Designer*
Bruce Rushin · *Alloy* Cupro-nickel & Nickel-brass · *Diameter*
28.4mm · *Weight* 12g · *Edge Thickness* 2.5mm · *Compositions*
75% Copper, 25% Nickel; 76% Copper, 4% Nickel, 20% Zinc.

£1 Edge Inscription *Decus Et Tutamen* · *Alloy* Nickel-brass
Diameter 22.5mm · *Weight* 9.5g · *Edge Thickness* 3.15mm
Composition 70% Copper, 5.5% Nickel, 24.5% Zinc.

50p *Designer* Christopher Ironside · *Alloy* Cupro-nickel · *Weight* 8g
Diameter 27.3mm · *Edge Thickness* 1.78mm
Composition 75% Copper, 25% Nickel.

20p *Designer* William Gardner · *Alloy* Cupro-nickel · *Weight* 5g
Diameter 21.4mm · *Edge Thickness* 1.7mm
Composition 84% Copper, 16% Nickel.

10p *Designer* Christopher Ironside · *Alloy* Cupro-nickel · *Weight* 6.5g
Diameter 24.5mm · *Edge Thickness:* 1.85mm
Composition 75% Copper, 25% Nickel.

5p *Designer* Christopher Ironside · *Alloy* Cupro-nickel
Weight 3.25g · *Diameter* 18.0mm *Edge Thickness* 1.7mm
Composition 75% Copper, 25% Nickel.

2p *Designer* Christopher Ironside · *Alloy* Copper-plated steel
Weight 7.12g · *Diameter* 25.9mm
Edge Thickness 1.85 mm/2.03mm · *Composition* Copper-plated steel.

1p *Designer* Christopher Ironside · *Weight* 3.56g · *Diameter* 20.° mm
Edge Thickness: 1.65mm · *Alloy* Copper-plated steel
Composition Copper-plated steel.

——— US POSTAL SERVICE'S UNOFFICIAL MOTTO ———

*'Neither snow nor rain nor heat nor gloom of night stays these couriers
from the swift completion of their appointed rounds.'*

Inscription found on New York's General Post Office (8th & 33rd),
thought to originate from Herodotus' description of the Persian couriers
*c.*500BC, translated by Professor George H. Palmer of Harvard University.
Contrary to popular belief, the motto has no official link with the USPS.

SOME PALMISTRY LINES

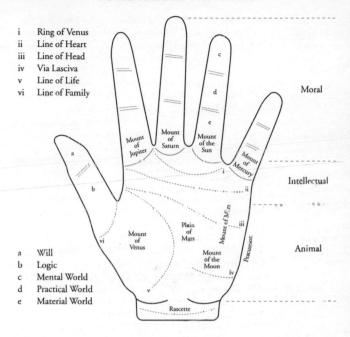

i   Ring of Venus
ii   Line of Heart
iii   Line of Head
iv   Via Lasciva
v   Line of Life
vi   Line of Family

a   Will
b   Logic
c   Mental World
d   Practical World
e   Material World

LAWS OF ROBOTICS

Although hinted at in some of his earlier works, Isaac Asimov's famous 3 Laws of Robotics were first explicitly stated in his 1942 story *Runaround*.

FIRST	SECOND	THIRD	ZEROTH
A robot may not injure a human being or, through inaction, allow a human being to come to harm.	*A robot must obey orders given it by human beings except where such orders would conflict with the 1st Law.*	*A robot must protect its own existence as long as such protection does not conflict with the 1st or 2nd Law.*	*A robot may not injure humanity or, through inaction, allow humanity to come to harm.*

Asimov later felt that his initial three laws were insufficient to protect society at large. Consequently, in his 1985 book *Robots and Empire*, he created a prequel, 'Zeroth' law, to which the other laws were subordinate.

THE DEMON'S DICTIONARY

Ambrose Bierce (1842–*c.*1914), was a remarkable man: a veteran of the American Civil War, a writer, poet, journalist, and – most memorably – the creator of *The Demon's Dictionary*. The caustic and cynical definitions of 'The American Swift' survive the test of time, and still speak to his intended audience: 'enlightened souls who prefer dry wines to sweet, sense to sentiment, wit to humour, and clean English to slang'. Shown below are some of the more pungent entries from *The Demon's Dictionary*.

ACHIEVEMENT · The death of endeavour and the birth of disgust.

ACTUALLY · Perhaps; possibly.

ADORE · To venerate expectantly.

ARMOUR · The kind of clothing worn by a man whose tailor is a blacksmith.

AUCTIONEER · A man who proclaims with a hammer that he has picked a pocket with his tongue.

BAROMETER · An ingenious instrument which indicates what kind of weather we are having.

BORE · A person who talks when you wish him to listen.

COURT FOOL · The plaintiff.

COWARD · One who in a perilous emergency thinks with his legs.

DENTIST · A prestidigitator who, putting metal into your mouth, pulls coins out of your pocket.

ENVELOPE · The coffin of a document; the scabbard of a bill; the husk of a remittance; the bedgown of a love-letter.

ERUDITION · Dust shaken out of a book into an empty skull.

FAMOUS · Conspicuously miserable.

FIDELITY · A virtue peculiar to those who are about to be betrayed.

FOREFINGER · The finger commonly used in pointing out two malefactors.

FROG · A reptile with edible legs.

GHOST · The outward and visible sign of an inward fear.

HABIT · A shackle for the free.

HERMIT · A person whose vices and follies are not sociable.

HOPE · Desire and expectation rolled into one.

HOSPITALITY · The virtue which induces us to feed and lodge certain persons who are not in need of food and lodging.

ILLUSTRIOUS · Suitably placed for the shafts of malice, envy and detraction.

———————— THE DEMON'S DICTIONARY cont. ————————

IMPIETY · Your irreverence toward my deity.

INFLUENCE · In politics, a visionary *quo* given in exchange for a substantial *quid.*

INSURRECTION · An unsuccessful revolution. Disaffection's failure to substitute misrule for bad government.

KILT · A costume sometimes worn by Scotchmen in America and Americans in Scotland.

LANGUAGE · The music with which we charm the serpents guarding another's treasure.

LITIGATION · A machine which you go into as a pig and come out of as a sausage.

MAUSOLEUM · The final and funniest folly of the rich.

MISFORTUNE · The kind of fortune that never misses.

PAINTING · The art of protecting flat surfaces from the weather and exposing them to the critic.

POLITICS · The conduct of public affairs for private advantage.

PRAY · To ask that the laws of the universe be annulled in behalf of a single petitioner confessedly unworthy.

PRICE · Value, plus a reasonable sum for the wear and tear of conscience in demanding it.

RIOT · A popular entertainment given to the military by innocent bystanders.

SATIETY · The feeling that one has for the plate after he has eaten its contents.

SELF-EVIDENT · Evident to one's self and to nobody else.

TELEPHONE · An invention of the devil which abrogates some of the advantages of making a disagreeable person keep his distance.

TWICE · Once too often.

ZEAL · A certain nervous disorder afflicting the young and inexperienced.

———————— SOME CHEMICAL ACRONYMS ————————

TCP	Trichlorophenylmethyliodosalicyl	*germicide*
TNT	2,4,6-Trinitrotoluene	*explosive*
PCP	Phencyclidine	*amphetamine*
LSD	d-Lysergic Acid Diethylamide	*hallucinogen*
DDT	Dichlorodiphenyltrichloroethane	*pesticide*
GTN	Glyceryl Trinitrate	*cardiac medication*

-------------------- SOME MEDICAL SHORTHAND --------------------

AAA...abdominal aortic aneurysm
ac ....before food
AD............Alzheimer's disease
AE........................air entry
AS ....aortic stenosis
AXR..............abdominal X-ray
bd.......................twice daily
B(N)O..........bowels (not) open
BP.................blood pressure
BS ....breath sounds
CN I–XII......cranial nerves 1–12
CP ....chest pain
CSU ....catheter stream urine
CT.....computerised tomography
CVA......cerebrovascular accident
CXR ....chest X-ray
D&V .....diarrhoea and vomiting
DTP.diphtheria, tetanus, pertussis
DVT ....deep vein thrombosis
EDD....estimated date of delivery
EMU ....early morning urine
FBC ....full blood count
FHx.................family history
Hb....................haemoglobin
HIB ..Haemophilus influenzae (b)
HPc..................history of Pc
HS ....heart sounds
Ht ....haematocrit
Ix ....investigations
JPS ....joint position sense
JVP.......jugular venous pressure
KUB ..kidneys, ureters, & bladder
LFTs ....liver function tests
LMP.........last menstrual period
LOC ....loss of consciousness
LT ....light touch
mane..............in the morning
MCS......microscopy, culture, &
sensitivity
MCV ...mean corpuscular volume
MI ....myocardial infarction
MMR ....measles, mumps, rubella
MRI..magnetic resonance imaging

MS ....multiple sclerosis
MSU ....mid-stream urine
N&V ....nausea and vomiting
nocte......................at night
NPL ....no perception of light
OCP ....oral contraceptive pill
OD ....once daily
ODQ.......on direct questioning
o/e................on examination
OTC..............over the counter
Pc...........presenting complaint
PMHx ....past medical history
PN ....percussion note
PND ....paroxysmal nocturnal
dyspnoea (waking SOB)
POM ..prescription only medicine
PP...............peripheral pulses
PR ....per rectum
prn...............when required
PSM ....pan-systolic murmur
PU...................passing urine
qds...............four times a day
RBC ....red blood count
RTA ....road traffic accident
Rx.........treatment, prescription
s/c....................sub-cutaneous
SHx.................social history
SI ....sexual intercourse
SL......................sub-lingual
SOA.............swelling of ankles
SOB ....shortness of breath
SOBAR...............SOB at rest
SOBOE...........SOB on exertion
TB ....tuberculosis
tds...............three times a day
TIA.....transient ischaemic attack
U&E.........urea and electrolytes
USA ....unstable angina
USS ....ultrasound scan
WR.........Wassermann reaction
x/7.................number of days
x/12...........number of months
x/52.............number of weeks

------------------ THE STATUE OF LIBERTY ------------------

Ground to tip of torch	305'1"	Distance across the eye	2'6"
Heel to top of head	111'1"	Length of nose	4'6"
Length of hand	16'5"	Length of right arm	42'0"
Index finger	8'0"	Thickness of right arm	12'0"
Chin to cranium	17'3"	Thickness of waist	35'0"
Ear to ear	10'0"	Total statue weight	225 tons
Width of mouth	3'0"	Steps to the Crown	354

Give me your tired, your poor, your huddled masses
yearning to breathe free, The wretched refuse of your
teeming shore, Send these, the homeless, tempest-tossed,
to me: I lift my lamp beside the golden door.

— Pedestal Inscription, EMMA LAZARUS, 1883

------------------ HORSEPOWER ------------------

Devised by James Watt (1736–1819), Horsepower is the power required to lift 550 pounds by 1 foot in 1 second: 33,000 foot-pounds per minute. 1 Horsepower = 745.7 watts; or 2,545 BTUs (British Thermal Units) per hour.

------------------ FOOTBALL WORLD CUP ------------------

YEAR	HOST	MASCOT	FINAL LINE UP	SCORE
1930	Uruguay	N/A	Uruguay *beat* Argentina	4-2
1934	Italy	N/A	Italy *beat* Czechoslovakia	2-1
1938	France	N/A	Italy *beat* Hungary	4-2
1950	Brazil	N/A	Uruguay *beat* Brazil	2-1
1954	Switzerland	N/A	W. Germany *beat* Hungary	3-2
1958	Sweden	N/A	Brazil *beat* Sweden	5-2
1962	Chile	N/A	Brazil *beat* Czechoslovakia	3-1
1966	England	Willie	England *beat* W. Germany	4-2
1970	Mexico	Juanito	Brazil *beat* Italy	4-1
1974	W. Germany	Tip & Tap	W. Germany *beat* Holland	2-1
1978	Argentina	Gauchito	Argentina *beat* Holland	3-1
1982	Spain	Naranjito	Italy *beat* W. Germany	3-1
1986	Mexico	Pique	Argentina *beat* W. Germany	3-2
1990	Italy	Ciao	Germany *beat* Argentina	1-0
1994	USA	Striker	Brazil *beat* Italy [on penalties]	3-2
1998	France	Footix	France *beat* Brazil	3-0
2002	Japan/S.Korea	Kaz, Ato, Nik	Brazil *beat* Germany	2-0

THE RIOT ACT

'Our Sovereign Lord the King chargeth and commandeth all persons, being assembled, immediately to disperse themselves, and peaceably to depart to their habitations, or to their lawful business, upon the pains contained in the Act made in the first year of King George the First for preventing tumults and riotous assemblies. God Save the King.'

Under the Riot Act 1714, once a magistrate had read this passage within the hearing of a crowd greater than twelve, the 'rioters' had one hour to disperse before their presence ceased to be a misdemeanour and became a felony, ultimately punishable by death. The wording had to be read exactly as written, since at least one conviction was overturned because *'God Save the King'* had been left out. The Riot Act was repealed in 1973.

PROVERBIALLY, YOU CAN'T

... have it both ways
... have your cake and eat it[†]
... get blood out of a stone
... make an omelette without breaking eggs
... make a silk purse out of a sow's ear
... run with the hare and hunt with the hounds
... teach an old dog new tricks
... tell a book by its cover
... shake hands with a clenched fist
... tell which way the train went, by looking at the track
... win arguments by interrupting speakers
... have a rainbow without rain
... pick up two melons with one hand
... fool all of the people all of the time
... sip soup with a knife
... see the sky through a bamboo tube
... measure the sea with a shell
... cheat an honest man
... catch a cub without going into the tiger's den

[†]There is a school of thought that maintains 'you can't eat your cake and have it' is a more logical construction.

NATO COUNTRIES

Belgium · Canada · Czech Rep. · Denmark · France · Germany · Greece
Hungary · Iceland · Italy · Luxembourg · Netherlands · Norway
Poland · Portugal · Spain · Turkey · United Kingdom · United States

OFFICIAL FLYING OF THE UNION FLAG

Queen's Accession..6th February
Prince Andrew's Birthday....................................19th February
St David's Day [Wales]...1st March
Prince Edward's Birthday ....10th March
Commonwealth Day ....2nd Monday in March
Queen's Birthday...21st April
St George's Day [England].....................................23rd April
Europe Day...9th May
Coronation Day...2nd June
Duke of Edinburgh's Birthday ....10th June
Queen's Official Birthday..................................June [varies]
Princess Anne's Birthday......................................15th August
Remembrance Sunday........................November [varies]
Prince of Wales' Birthday ....14th November
Queen's Wedding Day ....20th November
St Andrew's Day [Scotland] ....30th November

Also the Opening & Prorogation of Parliament. The Union Flag is flown from 8am–sunset.

MONDAY'S CHILD

Monday's child is fair of face,
Tuesday's child is full of grace,
Wednesday's child is full of woe,
Thursday's child has far to go,
Friday's child is loving and giving,
Saturday's child works hard for his living,
And, the child that is born on the Sabbath day
is bonny, blithe, good, and gay.

HOLALPHABETIC SENTENCES

*Also known as Pangrams, these are sentences containing every letter of the
alphabet, of particular interest to typographers when browsing fonts.*

The quick brown fox jumps over the lazy dog
Waltz, bad nymph, for quick jigs vex
How piqued gymnasts can level six jumping razorback frogs
We promptly judged antique ivory buckles for the next prize
Sixty zippers were quickly picked from the woven jute bag
Jump by vow of quick, lazy strength in Oxford
Jackdaws love my big sphinx of quartz

—————————— 'AVERAGES' ——————————

With the following list of values: 10, 10, 20, 30, 30, 30, 40, 50, 70, 100

MEAN .... the sum divided by the number of values 39
MODE .... the most popular value 30
MEDIAN .... the 'middle' value, here: (30+30) / 2 30
RANGE.... the difference between the highest & lowest value 90

— RADIO 10 CODES —

10–1 .... signal weak
10–2 .... signal good
10–3 .... stop transmitting
10–4 .... affirmative, ok
10–5 .... relay to
10–6 .... busy
10–7 .... out of service
10–9 .... repeat
10–10 .... negative
10–12 .... stand by
10–13 .... existing conditions
10–14 ..... message/information
10–15 .... message delivered
10–16 .... reply to message
10–18 .... urgent
10–19 .... (in) contact
10–20 .... location
10–21 .... telephone
10–22 .... disregard
10–23 .... arrived at scene
10–25 .... report to
10–26 .. estimated time of arrival
10–27 .... licence details
10–29 .... records check
10–30 .... danger/caution
10–31 .... pick up
10–33 .... urgent assistance

— NATO ALPHABET —

A	Alpha	N	November
B	Bravo	O	Oscar
C	Charlie	P	Papa
D	Delta	Q	Quebec
E	Echo	R	Romeo
F	Foxtrot	S	Sierra
G	Golf	T	Tango
H	Hotel	U	Uniform
I	India	V	Victor
J	Juliet	W	Whisky
K	Kilo	X	X-ray
L	Lima	Y	Yankee
M	Mike	Z	Zulu

— PHONETIC DIGITS —

0... Nadazero .... *nah-dah-zer-roh*
1... Unaone .... *oo-nah-wun*
2... Bissotwo .... *bee-soh-too*
3... Terrathree .... *tey-rah-tree*
4... Kartefour .... *kar-tay-fower*
5... Pantafive .... *pan-tah-five*
6... Soxisix .... *sok-see-six*
7... Setteseven .... *say-tay-seven*
8... Oktoeight .... *ok-tow-ait*
9... Novenine......... *no-vey-nine*

—————————— DRACONIAN ——————————

The term *Draconian* derives from DRACO, the Archon at Athens *c*.621BC.
Draco's laws, 'written in blood', prescribed death for even trivial crimes.

MOHS SCALE

In 1822, F. Mohs, an Austrian mineralogist, developed a scale to compare the hardness of substances relative to a selection of 10 different minerals, each of which is harder and thus capable of scratching its predecessor:

[1] Talc · [2] Gypsum · [3] Calcite · [4] Fluorite · [5] Apatite
[6] Orthoclase · [7] Quartz · [8] Topaz · [9] Corundum · [10] Diamond

PANTAGRUEL'S LABOURS

Rabelais' Gargantua demanded of his son Pantagruel the following toil:

66 *I intend and insist that you learn all languages perfectly; first of all Greek, in Quintilian's method; then Latin, then Hebrew, then Arabic and Chaldee. I wish you to form your style of Greek on the model of Plato, and of Latin on that of Cicero. Let there be no history you have not at your fingers' ends, and study thoroughly cosmography and geography. Of liberal arts, such as geometry, mathematics, and music, I gave you a taste when not above five years old, and I would have you now master them fully. Study astronomy, but not divination and judicial astrology, which I consider mere vanities. As for civil law, I would have thee know the digests by heart. You should also have a perfect knowledge of the works of Nature, so that there is no sea, river, or smallest stream, which you do not know for what fish it is noted, whence it proceeds, and whither it directs its course; all fowls of the air, all shrubs and trees whether forest or orchard, all herbs and flowers, all metals and stones, should be mastered by you. Fail not at the same time most carefully to peruse the Talmudists and Cabalists, and be sure by frequent anatomies to gain a perfect knowledge of that other world called the microcosm, which is man. Master these in your young days, and let nothing be superficial; as you grow into manhood you must learn chivalry, warfare, and field manœuvres.* **99**

ANTIQUARIAN BOOK ABBREVIATIONS

an	as new	dj	dust-jacket
f	fine: no defects	ep	endpapers
nf	near fine: slight wear	ge	gilt edges
vg	very good; some defects	htvb	Hors Texte, versos blank
g	good; average used book	insc	inscribed
ads	book includes adverts	lp	large paper edition
aeg	all edges gilt	op	out of print
cl	cloth	rem	remainder
dec	decorated	teg	top edge gilt

A FOR 'ORSES

A....................for 'orses	N....................for lope
B....................for mutton	O..........for the wings of a dove
C....................for miles	P....................for ming seals
D....................for dentures	Q....................for snooker
E..............for ning standard	R....................for mo
F....................for vessence	S....................for midable
G....................for police	T....................for two
H....................for consent	U....................for mizzam
I....................for Novello	V....................for la France
J....................for oranges	W....................for quits
K....................for teria	X....................for breakfast
L....................for leather	Y....................for mistress
M....................for sis	Z....................for breezes

---
ATMOSPHERIC LAYERS

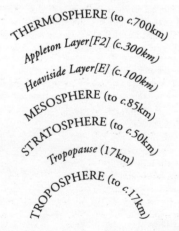

EXOSPHERE

THERMOSPHERE (to *c.*700km)

Appleton Layer[F2] (c.300km)

Heaviside Layer[E] (c.100km)

MESOSPHERE (to *c.*85km)

STRATOSPHERE (to *c.*50km)

Tropopause (17km)

TROPOSPHERE (to *c.*17km)

The Ozone Layer is located in the Stratosphere, between *c.*19–30km above the surface of the Earth. Ozone is created when energetic solar radiation strikes molecules of oxygen and causes the oxygen atoms to split apart. These atoms can then reform with O_2 molecules to form ozone (O_3): a process known as photolysis. Ozone absorbs the majority of solar UV radiation [290–400nm] some of which can be harmful to life on Earth.

THE ARAB LEAGUE

The Arab League, or the League of Arab States, was founded in Cairo in 1945 to 'promote economic, social, political, and military cooperation'.

Algeria · Bahrain · Comoros · Djibouti · Egypt · Iraq · Jordan
Kuwait · Lebanon · Libya · Mauritania · Morocco · Oman · Palestine
Qatar · Saudi Arabia · Somalia · Sudan · Syria · Tunisia
United Arab Emirates · Yemen

LEGAL DEPOSIT LIBRARIES

The British Library
Bodleian Library, Oxford
The University Library, Cambridge
The National Library of Scotland, Edinburgh
The Library of Trinity College, Dublin
The National Library of Wales, Aberystwyth

Under the terms of the Copyright Act 1911, and the Irish Copyright Act 1963, the British Library must be supplied with a copy of every work published in the UK and Republic of Ireland within a month. The five remaining Legal Deposit Libraries are entitled to request a free copy of every work within one year of publication.

DATING ABBREVIATIONS

SOH	sense of humour	SPARK	single parent raising kids
GSOH	good sense of humour	NLP	no losers please
WLTM	would like to meet	NUMP	no ugly men please
NTW	no time wasters	WMP	woo me please
LTR	long-term relationship	ANI	age not important
OHAC	own house and car	GRO	genuine replies only
PA	photograph appreciated	NS	non-smoker
ALA	all letters answered	(A)NI	(age) not important
BHM	big handsome man	LTM	longing to meet
SWF	single white female	WTT	willing to travel
SWM	single white male	DTE	down to earth
SBF	single black female	FS	friendship
SBM	single black male	ISO	in search of
SAF	single Asian female	SD	social drinker
SAM	single Asian male	4TLC	for tender loving care
DWM	divorced white male	VGL	very good looking

─────WINE BOTTLE NOMENCLATURE─────

Bottle Name	Champagne	Bordeaux	Burgundy
Picolo	¼	NA	NA
Chopine	NA	⅓	NA
Filette / Demi	½	½	½
Magnum	2	2	2
Marie Jeanne	NA	3	NA
Double Magnum	NA	4	NA
Jeroboam	4	6	4
Rehoboam	6	NA	6
Imperial	NA	8	NA
Methuselah	8	NA	8
Salmanazar	12	NA	12
Balthazar	16	16	16
Nebuchadnezzar	20	20	20
Melchior	24	24	24

Wine is usually matured in bottles no larger than a Magnum.

─────TECHNIQUES OF DIVINATION─────

observing facial features	anthroposcopy
analysing currents of water	bletonism
studying the passage of smoke	capnomancy
behaviour of birds	augury
looking into fire	pyromancy
examination of arrows	belomancy
interpreting oil poured on water	leconomancy
studying the entrails of animals	haruspicy
shadows or ghosts	sciomancy
examination of ashes	spodomancy
studying bones	osteomancy
analysis of numbers	arithmancy
interpretation of random (often biblical) texts	bibliomancy
becoming dizzy and falling	gyromancy
looking at fountains and springs	pegomancy
randomly drawing lots	sortilege
studying patterns in the flight of birds	ornithomancy
observation of lights or candles	lampadomancy
examining the entrails of sacrificial victims	hieroscopia
interpretation of laughter	geloscopy
burning straw on hot iron	sideromancy
analysis of pebbles	pessomancy

GLASGOW COMA SCALE

The Glasgow Coma Scale (GCS) was devised to help doctors assess the severity of head trauma and, importantly, to help track progress over time. The GCS is comprised of the sum of three tests: eye, verbal, and motor responses. The lowest possible GCS score is 3; the highest is 15.

BEST EYE RESPONSE	BEST MOTOR RESPONSE
1 . . . . No eye opening	1 . . . . No motor response
2 . . . . Eye opening to pain	2 . . . . Extension to pain
3 . . . . Eye opening to speech	3 . . . . Flexion to pain
4 . . . . Eyes open spontaneously	4 . . . . Withdraws from pain
	5 . . . . Localises pain
BEST VERBAL RESPONSE	6 . . . . Obeys commands
1 . . . . No verbal response	
2 . . . . Incomprehensible sounds	*To provide medics with additional*
3 . . . . Inappropriate words	*detail, the GCS is often expressed as*
4 . . . . Confused	*its three components, for example:*
5 . . . . Orientated	GCS 9 = E2 V4 M3

EVENTS OF THE DECATHLON

first day – 100 metres · long jump · shot put · high jump · 400 metres
second day – 110-metre hurdles · discus throw · pole vault
javelin throw · 1500 metres

EUCLIDEAN AXIOMS & POSTULATES

Things equal to the same thing are also equal to one another.

If equals are added to equals, the sums are equal.

If equals are subtracted from equals, the remainders are equal.

Things that coincide with one another are equal to one another.

The whole is greater than a part.

It is possible to draw a straight line from any point to any other point.

Any straight line can be infinitely extended.

It is possible to describe a circle with any centre and any radius.

All right angles are equal to one another.

If a straight line falling on two straight lines makes the interior angles on the same side less than two right angles, the straight lines, if produced indefinitely, will meet on that side on which the angles are less than the two right angles.

—AIRPORT MARSHALLING SIGNALS—

THIS WAY

ALL CLEAR

START ENGINES

PULL CHOCKS

INSERT CHOCKS

PROCEED

TURN RIGHT

TURN LEFT

SLOW DOWN

STOP

COME AHEAD

STOP ENGINES

——— PATRON SAINTS ———

Barbers	St Louis	Tax collectors	St Matthew
Artists & creatives	St Luke	Broadcasters	St Gabriel
Cobblers	St Crispin	Horses	St Giles
Florists	St Dorothea	Dairymaids	St Brigid
Editors	St John Bosco	Taxi-drivers	St Fiacre
Sculptors	St Claude	Librarians	St Jerome
Tailors	St Homobonus	Pilgrims	St Mennas, St James
Wine growers	St Joseph	Singers	St Cecilia
Pin makers	St Sebastian	Invalids	St Roche
Lighthouse keepers	St Venerius	Bricklayers	St Stephen
Bee keepers	St Ambrose	Children	St Nicholas
Speleologists	St Benedict	Miners	St Barbara
Gravediggers	St Anthony	Syphilitics	St George
Bakers	St Honoratus	Hoteliers	St Armand, St Julien
Domestic servants	St Zita	Diplomats	St Gabriel

GRAND NATIONAL WINNERS

Year	Weight	Odds	Winning Horse	Owner
1973	10-5	9/1	Red Rum	Noel Le Mare
1974	12-0	11/1	Red Rum	Noel Le Mare
1975	11-3	13/2	L'Escargot	Raymond Guest
1976	10-12	14/1	Rag Trade	Pierre Raymond
1977	11-8	9/1	Red Rum	Noel Le Mare
1978	10-9	14/1	Lucius	Fiona Whitaker
1979	10-0	25/1	Rubstic	John Douglas
1980	10-12	40/1	Ben Nevis	Redmond C. Stewart Jnr.
1981	10-13	10/1	Aldaniti	Nick Embiricos
1982	11-5	7/1	Grittar	Frank Gilman
1983	11-4	13/1	Corbiere	Bryan Burrough
1984	10-2	13/1	Hallo Dandy	Richard Shaw
1985	10-5	50/1	Last Suspect	Anne, Duchess of Westminster
1986	10-11	15/2	West Tip	Peter Luff
1987	10-13	28/1	Maori Venture	Jim Joel
1988	11-0	10/1	Rhyme 'n' Reason	Juliet Reed
1989	10-3	28/1	Little Polveir	Edward Harvey
1990	10-6	16/1	Mr. Frisk	Lois Duffey
1991	10-6	12/1	Seagram	Sir Eric Parker
1992	10-7	14/1	Party Politics	Patricia Thompson
1993	*Declared void after two false starts, though Easha Ness came in first.*			
1994	10-8	16/1	Miinnehoma	Freddie Starr
1995	10-6	40/1	Royal Athlete	Garry and Libby Johnson
1996	10-7	7/1	Rough Quest	Andrew Wates
1997	10-0	14/1	Lord Gyllene	Mr Stanley
1998	10-5	7/1	Earth Summit	Summit Partnership
1999	10-0	10/1	Bobbyjo	Bobby Burke
2000	10-12	10/1	Papillon	Norman Williamson
2001	10-12	33/1	Red Marauder	Norman Mason
2002	10-4	20/1	Bindaree	Raymond Mould

FIREWORK CATEGORIES

Category 1	Indoor fireworks. Small fireworks for use in restricted areas.
Category 2	Garden fireworks. For small displays; a minimum of 5 metres clearance for spectators.
Category 3	Display fireworks. A minimum of 25 metres clearance for spectators.
Category 4	Professional fireworks. Not suitable for use by the general public. A special licence is required.

—— CATEGORIES OF NOMENCLATURE FOR —— PLANET & SATELLITE FEATURES

Since 1919, the International Astronomical Union (IAU) has been responsible for the nomenclature of planets and satellites and their features. A complex taxonomy for naming new discoveries has developed providing thematic, historic, and even poetic associations with astronomical bodies. By convention, no names with military, political, or religious significance are allowed (excepting political figures alive before the C19th), and no individual may be honoured until they have been dead for at least three years. The following tabulation gives a few examples of categories used to name features on planets and satellites.

OBJECT	FEATURE	NOMENCLATURE CATEGORY
MOON	*Large craters*	Scholars, artists, and scientists
	Small craters	Common first names
VENUS	*Lineae*	Goddesses of war
	Dunes	Goddesses of deserts
	Terrae	Goddesses of love
MERCURY	*Valleys*	Radio-telescope facilities
MARS	*Large valleys*	Names for Mars in various languages
SATELLITES OF SATURN	*Tethys*	People and places in Homer's *Odyssey*
	Titan	Displaced ancient cultures
	Hyperion	Deities of the Sun and Moon
SATELLITES OF URANUS	*Miranda*	Characters and places from Shakespeare
	Titania	Female Shakespeare characters
EUROPA	*Rough terrain*	Places from Celtic mythology
	Ring features	Celtic stone circles

—————— BIRTHSTONES ——————

January	Garnet	July	Ruby
February	Amethyst	August	Sardonyx, Agate
March	Bloodstone	September	Sapphire
April	Diamond	October	Opal
May	Emerald	November	Topaz
June	Pearl, Alexandrite	December	Turquoise

---------------------------------SUSHI--------------------------------

Akagai	pepitona clam	Masu	trout
Anago	sea eel	Nori	sheets of dried seaweed
Aoyagi	Japanese red clam	Ocha	green tea
Ebi	boiled jumbo prawn	Saba	mackerel
Fugu	puffer fish	Sake	salmon
Gari	sliced ginger garnish	Sashimi	raw fish, without rice
Hamachi	yellowtail tuna	Shoyu	soy sauce
Hirame	halibut	Sushi	sweetened, pickled rice
Ika	squid	Tako	octopus
Ikura	salmon roe	Tamago	sweet, light omelette
Kaibashira	large scallops	Tekka Maki	tuna & rice roll
Kani	cooked crab	Toro	fatty tuna
Kappa	cucumber	Unagi	freshwater eel
Kobashira	small scallops	Uni	sea urchin
Maguro	tuna	Wasabi	hot Japanese horseradish

---------- BAKER STREET IRREGULARS ----------

The Baker Street Irregulars were Sherlock Holmes' 'unofficial force': a
dozen London urchins, apparently headed by a boy named Wiggins.
Holmes paid each boy a shilling a day, with a guinea prize to anyone who
found the vital clue. Used by Holmes to search out information where he
or the Police would be conspicuous, the Irregulars appeared in only three
of the stories: *A Study In Scarlet, The Sign of Four,* and *The Crooked Man.*

---OLYMPIC SWIMMING POOL SPECIFICATIONS---

Length	50m	Lane width	2.5m
Width	25m	Water temperature	25°–28°C
Number of lanes	8	Light intensity	>1500 lux

-------------- UN SECRETARIES-GENERAL --------------

1946–52	Trygve Lie	*Norway*
1953–61	Dag Hammarskjöld	*Sweden*
1961–71	U Thant	*Burma*
1972–81	Kurt Waldheim	*Austria*
1982–91	Javier Pérez de Cuéllar	*Peru*
1992–96	Boutros Boutros-Ghali	*Egypt*
1997–	Kofi Annan	*Ghana*

—— PORTRAITS ON AMERICAN BANKNOTES ——

George Washington	$1	OBSOLETE NOTES	
Thomas Jefferson	$2	William McKinley	$500
Abraham Lincoln	$5	Grover Cleveland	$1,000
Alexander Hamilton	$10	James Madison	$5,000
Andrew Jackson	$20	Salmon P. Chase	$10,000
Ulysses S. Grant	$50	Woodrow Wilson	$100,000
Benjamin Franklin	$100	*[large bills used for Federal transactions]*	

—— CURIOUS DEATHS OF SOME BURMESE KINGS ——

THEINHKO killed by a farmer whose cucumbers he ate without permission (931 AD). Theinko's Queen, fearing civil disorder, smuggled the farmer into the royal palace and dressed him in royal robes. He was proclaimed King NYAUNG-U SAWRHAN, and was known as the 'Cucumber King'. He later transformed his cucumber plantation into a spacious and pleasant royal garden.

ANAWRAHTA gored by a buffalo during a military campaign. (1077)

UZANA trampled to death by an elephant. (1254)

NARATHIHAPATE forced at knife-point to take poison. (1287)

MINREKYAWSWA crushed to death by his own elephant. (1417)

RAZADARIT died after becoming entangled in the rope with which he was lassoing elephants. (1423)

TABINSHWETI beheaded by his chamberlains whilst searching for a fictitious white elephant. (1551)

NANDABAYIN laughed to death when informed, by a visiting Italian merchant, that Venice was a free state without a king. (1599)

—— THIN ICE ——

This table gives some idea of the theoretically 'safe' thickness of ice for different weights. Walking on any ice is absurdly dangerous: don't do it.

Load	Depth (")		
Single person on skis	1.5	Medium truck, 3.5 tons	9
Single person on foot	2.5	7 tons	10
Groups in single file	3	15 tons	15
Snowmobile	3	25 tons	20
Average car	7.5	45 tons	25
Large car; small truck	8	70 tons	30
		[The table assumes solid blue/black ice]	

———————————— 'I LOVE YOU' ————————————

Afrikaans . . . . Ek het jou lief
Arabic . . . . Ohhe-buk
Braille . . . . ⠊⠀⠇⠕⠧⠑⠀⠽⠕⠥
Burmese . . . . Nin ko nga chitde; Chit pa de
Cantonese . . . . Ngor oi ley
Catalan . . . . T'estimo
Chewa . . . . Noi makokonda
Dutch . . . . Ik hou van je
Esperanto . . . . Mi amas vin
Finnish . . . . Minä rakastan sinua
French . . . . Je t'aime
Gaelic (Scot) . . . . Tha gradh agam ort
German . . . . Ich liebe dich
Ancient Greek . . . . Se erotao
Gujarati . . . . Maney tamari satey pyar che
Hawaiian . . . . Aloha i'a au oe; Aloha au la o'e
Hebrew . . . . Ani ohev otach
Hindi . . . . Mai tumaha pyar karta hu
Italian . . . . Ti amo
Japanese . . . . Aishite imasu
Kurdish . . . . Khoshim awée
Latin . . . . Te amo
Lithuanian . . . . As tave myliu
Morse . . . . · · / · — · · — — — · · · — · / — · — — — — — · · —
Persian / Farsi . . . . Mahn dousett daram; Ushegheh-tam
Pig Latin . . . . Iway ovelay ouyay
Polish . . . . Kocham cie
Portuguese . . . . Eu te amo
Romanian . . . . Te ubesc
Russian . . . . Ya tebya lyublyu
Serbo-Croatian . . . . Volim te; Ljubim te
Shona . . . . Ndinoluda
Spanish . . . . Te amo
Swedish . . . . Jag älskar dig
Swiss German . . . . I Chaa di Gärn
Tagalog . . . . Iniibig kita; Mahal kita
Thai . . . . Phom Rak Khun
Tswana . . . . Keyagorata
Turkish . . . . Seni seviyorum
Urdu . . . . Mi-an aap say piyar karta hun
Welsh . . . . 'Rwy'n dy garu di
Yiddish . . . . Ikh hob dikh lib
Zulu . . . . Ngiya kuthanda

———————AMERICAN DINER SLANG———————

Adam 'n' Eve ... two poached eggs	gravel train .... sugar bowl
murphy .... potatoes	haemorrhage .... ketchup
splash of red .... tomato soup	sea dust .... salt
Adam's ale .... water	yum-yum .... sugar
wreck 'em .... scramble the eggs	in the alley ..... serve as a side dish
moo juice .... milk	java, joe .... coffee
belch water .... soda water	life-preserver .... doughnut
on wheels .... take-away	breath .... onions
bucket of hail .... glass of ice	looseners .... prunes

hounds on an island .... sausages on beans
put out the lights and cry .... liver and onions
bucket of cold mud .... portion of chocolate ice cream
shingles with a shimmy .... toast and jam
two cows, make them cry .... two hamburgers with onions
zeppelins in a fog .... sausages in mashed potatoes

burn the British .... toasted muffin	lumber .... a toothpick
clean up the kitchen .... hash	mike and 'ike ...... salt and pepper
on a raft .... on toast	no cow .... without milk
wreath .... cabbage	sand .... sugar
bridge .... four of anything	a squeeze .... orange juice
hold the hail .... no ice	side-arms .... salt and pepper
crowd .... two of anything	warts .... olives
Eve with a lid on .... apple pie	axle grease .... butter

—— SEVEN WONDERS OF THE ANCIENT WORLD ——

THE GREAT PYRAMID OF GIZA is the huge stone structure near the ancient city of Memphis, used as a tomb for the Egyptian Pharaoh Khufu.

THE HANGING GARDENS OF BABYLON built as part of the palace of King Nebuchadnezzar II on the banks of the Euphrates.

THE STATUE OF ZEUS AT OLYMPIA carved by the legendary sculptor Pheidias.

THE TEMPLE OF ARTEMIS AT EPHESUS built to honour the goddess of wilderness and hunting.

THE MAUSOLEUM AT HALICARNASSUS tomb constructed for King Maussollos, Persian satrap of Caria.

THE COLOSSUS OF RHODES giant statue of the sun-god Helios.

THE LIGHTHOUSE OF ALEXANDRIA built by the Ptolemies on the island of Pharos.

WORD PAIRINGS

floating wreckage	flotsam & jetsam	*items thrown off ships*
movement up and down	pitch & yaw	*movement side to side*
elbow flexor	biceps & triceps	*elbow extensor*
left-hand side facing forward	port & starboard	*right-hand side facing forward*
a high-range speaker	tweeter & woofer	*a bass-range speaker*
librettist	Gilbert & Sullivan	*composer*
destruction	rack & ruin	*destitution*
lengthways	warp & weft	*crossways*
descends	stalactite & stalagmite	*ascends*
sea monster	Scylla & Charybdis	*whirlpool*
horizontal axis	x & y	*vertical axis*
pianist	Chas & Dave	*guitarist*
milk solids	curds & whey	*milk liquids*
linear gear	rack & pinion	*circular gear*

HERALDIC COLOUR SYMBOLISM

Colour	Symbolic Meaning	Associated Gemstone	Heraldic Name	Astrological Association
Black	Prudence	Diamond	Sable	Saturn
White	Innocence	Pearl	Argent	Luna
Blood-red	Fortitude	Sardonyx	Sanguine	Dragon's tail
Blue	Fidelity	Sapphire	Azure	Jupiter
Green	Love	Emerald	Vert	Venus
Yellow	Faith	Topaz	Or	Sol
Purple	Temperance	Amethyst	Purpure	Mercury
Tawny	Joy	Jacinth	Tenney	Dragon's head

LAY vs MEDICAL TERMINOLOGY

Tummy rumbling	Borborygmy
Tennis elbow	Lateral epicondylitis
That thing at the back of the throat	Uvula
Athlete's foot	Tinea pedis
The ridge over the top lip	Philtrum
Fast pulse	Tachycardia
Housemaid's knee	Prepatellar bursitis
Squint	Strabismus
Bunions	Hallux valgus
That dent in the middle of the chest	Xiphisternum

—————— THE NATIONAL ANTHEM ——————

God save our gracious Queen!
Long live our noble Queen!
God save the Queen!
Send her victorious,
Happy and glorious,
Long to reign over us,
God save the Queen.

Thy choicest gifts in store,
On her be pleased to pour,
Long may she reign!
May she defend our laws,
And ever give us cause,
To sing with heart and voice,
God save the Queen!

O Lord God arise,
Scatter our enemies,
And make them fall!
Confound their knavish tricks,
Confuse their politics,
On you our hopes we fix,
God save the Queen!

Not in this land alone,
But be God's mercies known,
From shore to shore!
Lord make the nations see,
That men should brothers be,
And form one family,
The wide world o'er.

From every latent foe,
From the assassins blow,
God save the Queen!
O'er her thine arm extend,
For Britain's sake defend,
Our mother, prince, and friend,
God save the Queen!

Some claim the Anthem became linked with royal events in 1745, when it was played by the orchestra of the Theatre Royal, Drury Lane, to mark George II's defeat at Prestonpans by the forces of Bonnie Prince Charlie. By tradition, at royal occasions only the first verse is usually played.

—————— ARCHAIC GOLF CLUB NOMENCLATURE ——————

Few formal links exist between modern and ancient golf clubs, but the list below gives an approximate guide to what comparisons can be made:

Woods No. 1	Play Club, Driver	No. 4	Jigger, Mashie Iron
No. 2	Brassie	No. 5	Mashie
No. 3	Spoon	No. 6	Spade Mashie
No. 4	Baffy	No. 7	Mashie-Niblick
		No. 8	Pitching Mashie
Irons No. 1	Driving Iron, Cleek	No. 9	Niblick, Baffing Spoon
No. 2	Cleek, Midiron	No. 10	Wedge or Jigger
No. 3	Mid-Mashie	Blank	Putter

WWII RATIONING

Rationing fluctuated throughout the war as the food supply changed. Below is the basic *weekly* ration for an adult in 1942, although this was supplemented by a system of monthly points for additional purchases.

MEAT . . . . to the value of 1s.2d.	SUGAR 8oz, 225g
BACON & HAM 4oz, 100g	TEA 2oz, 50g
BUTTER 2oz, 50g	EGGS 1
CHEESE 2–8oz, 50–225g	*Monthly Ration*
MARGARINE 4oz, 100g	PRESERVES 1lb, 450g
COOKING FAT 4oz, 100g	DRIED EGGS 1pkt
MILK . . . . 2–3 pints	SWEETS 12oz, 350g

WEDDING ANNIVERSARIES

YEAR	BRITISH	AMERICAN	MODERN
1st	Cotton	Paper	Clocks
2nd	Paper	Cotton	China
3rd	Leather	Leather	Crystal
4th	Fruit, Flowers	Linen, Silk	Appliances
5th	Wood	Wood	Silverware
6th	Sugar	Iron	Wooden
7th	Wool, Copper	Wool, Copper	Desk items
8th	Bronze, Pottery	Bronze	Linens, Lace
9th	Pottery, Willow	Pottery	Leather
10th	Tin	Tin, Aluminium	Diamond
11th	Steel	Steel	Jewellery
12th	Silk, Linen	Silk	Pearls
13th	Lace	Lace	Textiles, furs
14th	Ivory	Ivory	Gold
15th	Crystal	Crystal	Watches
20th	China	China	Platinum
25th	Silver	Silver	Sterling silver
30th	Pearl	Pearl	Diamond
35th	Coral	Coral, Jade	Jade
40th	Ruby	Ruby	Ruby
45th	Sapphire	Sapphire	Sapphire
50th	Gold	Gold	Gold
55th	Emerald	Emerald	Emerald
60th	Diamond	Diamond	Diamond
70th	Platinum	Platinum	Platinum
75th	Diamond	Diamond	Diamond

ANTIQUARIAN PAPER SIZES

BOOK SIZES

Name	*Inches*
Foolscap octavo	6¾ x 4¼
Crown octavo	7½ x 5
Large post octavo	8¼ x 5¼
Demy octavo	8¾ x 5⅝
Medium octavo	9 x 5¾
Royal octavo	10 x 6¼
Imperial octavo	11 x 7½
Foolscap quarto	8½ x 6¾
Crown quarto	10 x 7½
Demy quarto	11¼ x 8¾
Medium quarto	11½ x 9
Royal quarto	12½ x 10
Imperial quarto	15 x 11
Foolscap folio	13½ x 8½
Crown folio	15 x 10
Royal folio	20 x 12½
Imperial folio	22 x 15

WRITING PAPER SIZES

Emperor	66 x 47
Antiquarian	53 x 31
Grand Eagle	28¾ x 42
Double Elephant	40 x 26¾
Colombier	34½ x 23½
Atlas	34 x 26
Double Large Post	33 x 21
Double Demy	35½ x 22½
Double Post	30½ x 19
Imperial	30 x 22
Elephant	28 x 23
Super Royal	27 x 19
Double Foolscap	27 x 16½
Cartridge	26 x 21½
Royal	24 x 19
Medium	22 x 17½
Large Post	20¾ x 16½
Copy (Draught)	20 x 16
Demy	20 x 15½
Post	18¾ x 15¼
Pinched Post	18½ x 14¾
Foolscap	17 x 13½
Brief	16½ x 13¼
Pott	15 x 12½

THE BEAUFORT SCALE

Beaufort Scale	Sea Height feet	Knots	MPH	Description
0	—	<1	<1	Calm
1	¼	1–3	1–3	Light air
2	½	4–6	4–7	Light breeze
3	2	7–10	8–12	Gentle breeze
4	3½	11–16	13–18	Moderate breeze
5	6	17–21	19–24	Fresh breeze
6	9½	22–27	25–31	Strong breeze
7	13½	28–33	32–38	Near gale
8	18	34–40	39–46	Gale
9	23	41–47	47–54	Strong gale
10	29	48–55	55–63	Storm
11	37	56–63	64–72	Violent storm
12	—	≥64	≥73	Hurricane

PHOBIAS

Amphibians	batrachophobia
Beards	pogonophobia
Deformity	teratophobia
Fall of satellites	keraunothnetophobia
Being tied up	merinthophobia
Being contagious	tapinophobia
Theft	harpaxophobia
Being stared at	ophthalmophobia
Tickling with feathers	pteronophobia
Sharks	selachophobia
Opening one's eyes	optophobia
Being touched	aphenphosmphobia
Blushing	ereuthophobia
Choking	pnigerophobia
Clowns	coulrophobia
Novelty	cainolophobia
Colours	chromatophobia
Detumescence	medomalacuphobia
Crossing bridges	gephyrophobia
Spiders	arachnophobia
Crowds	enochlophobia
Failure or defeat	kakorrhiaphobia
Being ridiculed	catagelophobia
Foreign languages	xenoglossophobia
Frogs	ranidaphobia
The skins of animals	doraphobia
Sea swell	cymobphobia
Garlic	alliumphobia
Getting wrinkles	rhytiphobia
Ghosts	phasmophobia
Going to school	didaskaleinophobia
Doctors	iatrophobia
Gold	aurophobia
Gravity	barophobia
Hair	trichopathophobia
Hell	stygiophobia
Voids	kenophobia
Imperfection	atelophobia
Itching	acarophobia
Kissing	philematophobia
People or society	anthropophobia
Snow	chionophobia
Wasps	spheksophobia

—————————— PUBLIC SCHOOL SLANG ——————————

In his remarkable 1900 text, *The Public School Word Book*, John Farmer set out to collect 'words, phrases, names, and allusions to customs as are now, or have been, *peculiar* to English public school life'. The table below offers a small, and expurgated, selection of some of these curious phrases:

ABROAD *(Winchester)* Convalescing, out of the sick room.

ATHENS *(Eton)* A bathing place.

BAT-MUGGER *(Winchester)* Wooden instrument used to oil cricket bats.

BEARDS! *(The Leys)* An exclamation of surprise.

BIBBLING *(Winchester)* 6 cane stokes.

BOSTRUCHYZER *(Oxford)* A small comb for curling the whiskers.

CHARLIES *(Winchester)* Thick gloves made of twine.

CHEESE *(Cambridge)* A dandy.

CHINNER *(Winchester)* A wide grin.

CLIPE *(general)* To tell tales.

COXY *(general)* Stuck up, conceited.

DEVOR *(Charterhouse)* Plum cake.

DRY BOB *(Eton)* A cricketer.

EX TRUMPS *(Winchester)* Extempore.

FLUKE *(general)* To shirk.

GOD *(Eton)* 6th-form boy.

GROUT *(Marlborough)* To swot.

MAJOR *(general)* An older brother.

MINOR *(general)* A younger brother.

MUTTONER *(Winchester)* A blow on the knuckles whilst batting.

MUZZ *(Westminster)* To read.

NESTOR *(Eton)* An undersized boy.

NEW BUG *(general)* New boy.

ON & OFF *(Tonbridge)* Lemonade.

PEMPE *(Winchester)* Imaginary object that a NEW BUG is sent to find.

PEPPER *(general)* To mark in the accents on a Greek exercise.

QUILL *(Winchester)* To flatter.

ROD MAKER *(Winchester)* The man who makes the rods for BIBBLING.

SAPPY *(Durham)* Severe caning.

SWIPES *(Stonyhurst)* The boy who serves beer at supper.

TACK *(Sherbourne)* A study feast.

TIZZYPOOLE *(general)* Fives ball.

WET BOB *(Eton)* A rower.

VARMINT *(general)* Good, spruce.

THE HAMPTON COURT MAZE

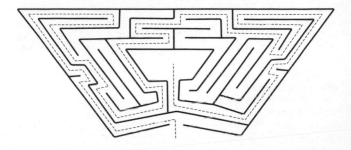

The maze at Hampton Court was planted sometime between 1689–95, by George London and Henry Wise, for William of Orange. It is thought the present design replaced an earlier maze of Wolsey's time. Originally constructed entirely from hornbeam, the maze has, over the years, been repaired and patched with a variety of different hedge types. Defoe called it 'a labyrinth', but really the maze is quite straightforward. As one writer noted, the maze 'is quite sufficient a puzzle to sustain interest and cause amusement, but without the needless and tedious excess of intricacy'. The maze occupies under ⅛ acre, and in total the walks stretch to about ½ mile.

GLOVE SIZES

Most traditional glove sizing dates back to the work of Grenoble-born Xavier Jouvin. In 1834, with the advent of accurate mechanised glove manufacture, Jouvin established a sizing system which was based on width of the knuckles. This system has survived metrification, and is still widely used, although there are differences between England and Europe:

English	6	6½	7	7½	8	8½	9	9½	10
Continental	6	7	8	9	10	11	12	13	14

The sleeve length of a glove is another consideration of sizing. Most gloves nowadays are worn very short, but for formal events much longer gloves are required. Sleeve length is often calculated by button length – a tradition which derives from the French technique of placing buttons an inch apart. So, a 4-button glove extends about 4 inches from the thumb. The following is a brief guide to the button lengths of some glove styles:

Shoulder length	20	Elbow	8
Above elbow	16	Mid-forearm	6

---------------- TWELVE DAYS OF CHRISTMAS ----------------

DAY	GIFTS FROM TRUE LOVE	CHRISTIAN INTERPRETATION
1st	A Partridge in a Pear Tree	*the One true God*
2nd	Two Turtle Doves	*the Old and New Testaments*
3rd	Three French Hens	*Faith, Hope, and Charity*
4th	Four Calling Birds	*the Four Gospels*
5th	Five Golden Rings	*the Books of Moses*
6th	Six Geese a-laying	*the six Days of Creation*
7th	Seven Swans a-swimming	*the seven gifts of the Holy Spirit*
8th	Eight Maids a-milking	*the eight Beatitudes*
9th	Nine Ladies Dancing	*the nine Fruits of the Spirit*
10th	Ten Lords a-leaping	*the Ten Commandments*
11th	Eleven Pipers Piping	*the eleven Faithful Apostles*
12th	Twelve Drummers Drumming	*the Apostles' Creed*

---------------- IVY LEAGUE UNIVERSITIES ----------------

Brown · Columbia · Cornell · Dartmouth
Harvard · Pennsylvania · Princeton · Yale

[The phrase is thought to have been coined by Stanley Woodward, sports-writer at the *New York Herald Tribune* in the early 1930s.]

---------------- CHRONOGRAMS ----------------

Chronograms, or eteostichons, are inscriptions or riddles in which certain letters, representing Roman numerals, stand for dates. Perhaps the most famous chronogram is that written on the death of Queen Elizabeth I:

My Day Closed Is In Immortality = MDCIII = 1603

The Great Fire of London was marked with the following eteostichon:

LorD haVe MerCI Vpon Vs = L+D+V+M+C+I+V+V= 1666

Addison denounced chronograms as 'the results of monkish ignorance' and sneered that 'tricks in writing require much time and little capacity'.

---------------- THE ROYAL PARKS ----------------

St James's Park · Hyde Park · Kensington Gardens · Greenwich Park
Bushy Park · Richmond Park · The Green Park · The Regent's Park

MONEY SLANG

£1	Quid, Nugget, Dollar	£50	Bull's eye
£5	Jack, Blue, Godiva	£100	Ton, Century
£10	Tenner, Pavarotti, Cock	£500	Monkey
£20	Score	£1000	Grand, Rio (Grande)
£25	Pony	£2000	Archer

YUPPIES

BOBO	Burnt Out But Opulent
BUPPIE	Black Upwardly-mobile Professional
DINKIE	Dual Income, No Kids
DINKY	Double Income, No Kids (Yet)
DUMP	Destitute Unemployed Mature Professional
GOLDIE	Golden Oldie, Lives Dangerously
GUPPIE	Green Upwardly-mobile Professional
LOMBARD	Lots Of Money But A Right Dickhead
NIMBY	Not In My Back Yard
OINK	One Income, No Kids
PIPPIE	Person Inheriting Parents' Property
PUPPIE	Poncy Upwardly-mobile Professional
SCUM	Self-Centred Urban Male
SILKY	Single Income, Loads of Kids
SINBAD	Single Income, No Boyfriend, Absolutely Desperate
SINK	Single, Independent, No Kids
SITCOM	Single Income, Two Children, Outrageous Mortgage
WOOPIE	Well-Off Older Person
YAPPIE	Young Affluent Parent
YUPPIE	Young Upwardly-mobile Professional Person

TONGUE TWISTERS

Eleven benevolent elephants · Preshrunk silk-shirt sale
Three short sword sheaths · An Argyle Gargoyle
Gobbling gargoyles gobbled gabbling goblins
I wish to wash my Irish wristwatch · Lovely lemon liniment

DEADLY SINS & CARDINAL VIRTUES

SINS — Pride · Greed · Lust · Envy · Gluttony · Anger · Sloth
VIRTUES — Prudence · Justice · Temperance · Fortitude

——————DEGREES OF FREEMASONRY——————

Though the subject of much speculation and denial, it is claimed by some
that Freemasonry employs the following thirty-three degree hierarchy:

1º	Entered Apprentice	1º
2º	Fellow Craft	2º
3º	Master Mason	3º
4º	Secret Master	4º
5º	Perfect Master	5º
6º	Intimate Secretary	6º
7º	Provost and Judge	7º
8º	Superintendent of the Building	8º
9º	Master Elect of Nine	9º
10º	Illustrious Master Elect of Fifteen	10º
11º	Sublime Knight, Chevalier Elect	11º
12º	Grand Master Architect	12º
13º	Royal Arch of Enoch	13º
14º	Scottish Knight of Perfection	14º
15º	Knight of the Sword & of The East	15º
16º	Prince of Jerusalem	16º
17º	Knight of the East & West	17º
18º	Knight of the Eagle & Pelican	18º
	and Sovereign Prince Rose Croix of Heredom	
19º	Grand Pontiff	19º
20º	Venerable Grand Master	20º
21º	Patriarch Noachite, Prussian Chevalier	21º
22º	Prince of Libanus, Royal Hatchet	22º
23º	Chief of the Tabernacle	23º
24º	Prince of the Tabernacle	24º
25º	Chevalier of the Brazen Serpent	25º
26º	Prince of Mercy	26º
27º	Grand Commander of the Temple	27º
28º	Knight of the Sun, Prince Adept	28º
29º	Knight of St Andrew	29º
30º	Grand Elected Knight Kadosh,	30º
	Knight of the Black and White Eagle	
31º	Grand Inspector Inquisitor Commander	31º
32º	Sublime Prince of the Royal Secret	32º
33º	Sovereign Grand Inspector General	33º

——————————THE SEVEN DWARVES——————————

Bashful · Doc · Dopey · Grumpy · Happy · Sleepy · Sneezy

TEST MATCH SPECIAL NICKNAMES

Johnners............Brian Johnston	*The Bearded Wonder*...Bill Frindall
Blowers..............Henry Blofeld	*Bumble* ....David Lloyd
Aggers.............Jonathan Agnew	*The Alderman* ....Don Mosey
CMJ...Christopher Martin-Jenkins	*The Boil*.............Trevor Bailey
ARL ....Tony Lewis	*Foxy*................Graeme Fowler

ROMAN NUMERALS

1	I	30	XXX	600	DC
2	II	40	XL	700	DCC
3	III	50	L	800	DCCC
4	IV	60	LX	900	CM
5	V	70	LXX	1,000	M
6	VI	80	LXXX	5,000	$\overline{V}$
7	VII	90	XC	10,000	$\overline{X}$
8	VIII	100	C	50,000	$\overline{L}$
9	IX	200	CC	100,000	$\overline{C}$
10	X	400	CD	500,000	$\overline{D}$
20	XX	500	D	1,000,000	$\overline{M}$

THE APOSTLES

Simon (Peter) · Andrew · James · John · Philip · Bartholomew
Thomas (Didymus) · Matthew · James · Thaddaeus
Simon the Zealot · Judas Iscariot · Matthias

SYSTEMS OF GOVERNMENT

rule by	*is called*		
all equally	pantisocracy	the people	democracy
armed forces	militocracy	the poor	ptochocracy
bishops	exarchy	pope	paparchy
civil servants	bureaucracy	propertied class	timocracy
clerics	ecclesiarchy	religious law	theocracy
elderly	gerontocracy	saints	hagiarchy
eldest male	patriarchy	slaves	doulocracy
judges	kritarchy	a small cabal	oligarchy
men	androcracy	technical experts	technocracy
nobility	aristocracy	wealthy	plutocracy
one individual	autocracy	women	gynarchy
		the worst possible	kakistocracy

——— SOME TYPOGRAPHICAL TERMS ———

LEAD(ING) The spacing between baselines of text. Originally from the strip of soft metal separating lines of type.

KERN(ING) Overhang of one letter to another which affects the spacing of characters. Kerning is altered to make text more clear.

To To

un-kerned   kerned

WORD SPACE The spacing added between words. This is usually equal when the right hand edge is ragged, but will vary when (as in this para) the text is set justified.

GUTTER Space between a number of columns, or between the text and the spine or edge.

DASHES There are three standard dashes: - (hyphen) – (en dash) — (em dash).

FONT TYPES San-serif, Serif, *script.*

LETTERSPACING The spacing between the letters of a word, sometimes varied to improve legibility. It is not the same as KERNING (which affects pairs of letters), and should be used sparingly. It is normally employed only with uppercase titling text because, as Frederic Goudy once said, 'a man who would letterspace lowercase text would steal sheep'.

LIGATURES The conflation of two characters to avoid collisions or to facilitate legibility, for example:

fi rather than fi

LINE WEIGHTS ¼ pt, ½ pt, 1–10pt

JUSTIFICATION The way in which text flows from left to right. Text can be left, right, or centre justified or, like this paragraph, fully justified so that it runs flush against both the left and right margin.

TYPE STRUCTURE

TYPOGRAPHICAL POINT SIZES

4 5 6 7 8 9 10 11 12 14 18 24 36 48

PAPER 'A' SIZES

A size	mm		
A10	26 x 37	A4	210 x 297
A9	37 x 52	A3	297 x 420
A8	52 x 74	A2	420 x 594
A7	74 x 105	A1	594 x 841
A6	105 x 148	A0	841 x 1189
A5	148 x 210	2A	1189 x 1682
		4A	1682 x 2378

HOW TO GET AN UPGRADE

Get an ink-stamp made from the
graphic shown and stamp it onto
the front of your airline tickets.
Seal the tickets in an envelope and
hand this over at the check-in desk
with an air of utter confidence.

DEWEY DECIMAL BOOK CLASSIFICATION

000–099	General works	500–599	Pure science
100–199	Philosophy	600–699	Technology
200–299	Religion	700–799	Arts
300–399	Social sciences	800–899	Literature
400–499	Language	900–999	Geography, History

395 Etiquette (Manners) · 399 Customs of war & diplomacy
441 French writing system & phonology · 648 Housekeeping
564 Fossil Mollusca & Molluscoidea · 624 Civil engineering
674 Lumber processing, wood products, cork

BLUE LIGHT USERS

*The Road Vehicle Licensing Regulations permit the following services to
display blue lights on their emergency vehicles:*

Police · Fire · Ambulance · Mountain Rescue
Coastguard · Mine Rescue · Human Tissue & Transplant
Forestry Commission Fire Service · Army Bomb Disposal
Naval Nuclear Monitoring · Blood Transfusion Services
RAF Armament Support · Royal National Lifeboat Institution

CARRY ON FILMS

Carry On ...	*Year*
Sergeant[†]	1958
Teacher[†]	1959
Nurse[†]	1959
Constable[†]	1960
Regardless[†]	1961
Cruising	1962
Cabby[†]	1963
Spying	1964
Jack	1964
Cleo	1964
Cowboy	1965
Screaming!	1966
Don't Lose Your Head	1966
Follow That Camel	1967
Doctor[†]	1968
Up the Khyber	1968
Camping[†]	1969
Again Doctor[†]	1969
Loving[†]	1970
Up the Jungle	1970
Henry	1971
At Your Convenience[†]	1971
Matron[†]	1972
Abroad[†]	1972
Girls	1973
Dick[†]	1974
Behind	1975
England	1976
Emmannuelle	1978
Columbus	1992

[† Indicates appearance by Hattie Jacques]

POKER HANDS & PROBABILITIES

1,098,240 ways	One pair	35 to 24
123,552 ways	Two pairs	20 to 1
54,912 ways	Three of a Kind	46 to 1
10,200 ways	Straight	254 to 1
5,108 ways	Flush	508 to 1
3,744 ways	Full House	693 to 1
624 ways	Four of a Kind	4,164 to 1
36 ways	Straight Flush	72,192 to 1
4 ways	Royal Flush	649,739 to 1

UNION FLAG COLOUR SPECS

	Pantone	*Web Safe*	*RGB* %s	*CMYK*
Union Flag Blue	280	#003399	0·13.5·39	100·72·0·18
Union Flag Red	186	#cc0000	85.9·11.7·13.8	0·91·76·6

THREE WISE MEN

MELCHIOR	King of Arabia	GOLD
CASPAR	King of Tarsus	FRANKINCENSE
BALTHAZAR	King of Ethiopia	MYRRH

WWII POSTAL ACRONYMS

B.U.R.M.A. .... Be Upstairs Ready My Angel
M.A.L.A.Y.A. .... My Ardent Lips Await Your Arrival
N.O.R.W.I.C.H. .... (K)nickers Off Ready When I Come Home
S.W.A.L.K. .... Sealed With A Loving Kiss
H.O.L.L.A.N.D. .... Hope Our Love Lasts And Never Dies
I.T.A.L.Y. .... I'm Thinking About Loving You
B.O.L.T.O.P .... Better On Lips Than On Paper

EMOTICONS

:-)	Hi	{:-)	Wearing a toupee
;-)	Winking	+-:-)	The Pope
:-(	Frown	:-Q	Smoker
:-I	Indifferent	;-?	Pipe-smoker
:->	Sarcastic	:-7	Cigar-smoker
>:->	Devilish	:-/	Sceptical
:-o	Wow!	C=:-)	Chef
:-C	Astonished!	@:-)	Wearing a turban
:-|	Grim	:-)8	Wearing a bow-tie
:,	Smirking	!-(	Black eye
:-||	Angry	5:-)	Elvis
:-x	Kissing	:,(	Crying
:-"	Pursed lips	=):-)=	Abraham Lincoln
:-#	My lips are sealed	%-)	Dazed
8-|	Amazement	*<:-)	Santa
>-<	Absolutely livid!	0:-)	Angel
:-}	Moustached	:( )	Bigmouth
(-:	Left-handed	:-#	Wearing braces
:*)	Drunk	:-@	Screaming
[:]	Robot	:-M	Speak no evil
8-)	Wearing sunglasses	:-Y	An aside
B:-)	Sunglasses on head	:-| :-|	Déjà vu
:-{}	Wearing lipstick	@}->--	Rose

SCORING CONKERS

As every school-boy knows, conker players alternate striking their
opponent's conker; each player receives three shots at a time. The game
ends when one of the conkers is smashed. A conker is scored by the
number of other conkers it has demolished. A new conker is always a
'one-er' – and its score increases by adding the score of its defeated
opponent. For example, if a 'one-er' smashes another 'one-er' it becomes
a 'two-er'. If a 'six-er' destroys a 'three-er' it becomes a 'nine-er'; and so on.

E-NUMBERS

100–199 . . . . food colours
200–299 . . . . preservatives
300–399 . . . . antioxidants, phosphates, and complexing agents
400–499 . . . . thickeners, gelling agents, phosphates, emulsifiers
500–599 . . . . salts and related compounds
600–699 . . . . flavour enhancers
700–899 . . . . *not used for human food additives*
900–999 . . . . surface-coating agents, gases, sweeteners
1000–1399 . . . . miscellaneous
1400–1499 . . . . starch derivatives

examples: E150a Plain Caramel · E175 Gold · E356 Sodium adipate
E219 Sodium methyl p-hydroxybenzoate · E948 Oxygen
E403 Ammonium alginate · E422 Glycerol · E553b Talc · E967 Xylitol

SEABREEZE

2 vodka · 3 cranberry juice · 2 grapefruit juice · lime peel
Shake all the ingredients with ice, and strain into a tall glass.

SGT. PEPPER

The following list contains some of those people whose images appeared
on Peter Blake's celebrated 1971 cover of The Beatles' *Sgt. Pepper* album.

Aleister Crowley	Tony Curtis	Marlon Brando
Mae West	Wallace Berman	Tom Mix
Lenny Bruce	Tommy Handley	Albert Einstein
Karlheinz Stockhausen	Marilyn Monroe	Oscar Wilde
W.C. Fields	William Burroughs	Tyrone Power
Carl Gustav Jung	Richard Lindner	Larry Bell
Edgar Allan Poe	Oliver Hardy	Johnny Weissmuller
Fred Astaire	Karl Marx	Stephen Crane
Richard Merkin	H.G. Wells	Issy Bonn
Huntz Hall	Stuart Sutcliffe	Albert Stubbins
Simon Rodia	Dylan Thomas	Lewis Carroll
Bob Dylan	Dion	T.E. Lawrence
Aubrey Beardsley	David Livingstone	Sonny Liston
Sir Robert Peel	Stan Laurel	Marlene Dietrich
Aldous Huxley	George Bernard Shaw	Diana Dors
Terry Southern	Max Miller	Shirley Temple

RNID MANUAL ALPHABET SIGNS

The National Bureau for Promoting the General Welfare of the Deaf was founded in 1911 by the merchant banker Leo Bonn, who was himself deaf. In 1924 the Bureau was renamed the National Institute for the Deaf; in 1958 the Duke of Edinburgh agreed to become its Patron; and during her 1961 Jubilee year the Queen granted the NID its Royal prefix.

TOASTS OF THE NAVY

Monday	OUR SHIPS AT SEA
Tuesday	OUR MEN
Wednesday	OURSELVES
Thursday	A BLOODY WAR OR A SICKLY SEASON
Friday	A WILLING FOE & SEA ROOM
Saturday	SWEETHEARTS & WIVES (MAY THEY NEVER MEET)
Sunday	ABSENT FRIENDS

——————— PALINDROMES ———————

Sotades of Maronea (*c.*275BC) is credited as one of the early inventors of the palindrome: words or phrases that read the same backwards as forwards. Sotades is thought to have employed the device in many of his writings – writings that were often so obscene and defamatory that finally, having insulted Ptolemy II, he was encased in lead and drowned.

Sums are not set as a test on Erasmus[†]
Go deliver a dare, vile dog!
Madam, in Eden I'm Adam
May a moody baby doom a yam?
Do geese see God?
Murder for a jar of red rum
Never odd or even
Satan, oscillate my metallic sonatas!
Dogma: I am God
Ah, Satan sees Natasha
Norma is as selfless as I am, Ron[†]
Anne, I vote more cars race Rome to Vienna
Some men interpret nine memos
Are we not drawn onward, we few, drawn onward to new era?
Able was I, ere I saw Elba
Too bad — I hid a boot
A man, a plan, a canal: Panama

[†]*Indicates that the palindrome has been attributed to W.H. Auden*

——————— THE ERINYES ———————

Three daughters of Gaia, created from the blood of Uranus when he was castrated by Cronus, the Erinyes (or Furies) of Greek myth, were the spirits of conscience, punishment, and retribution. The three Erinyes are:

MEGAERA · *the jealous*
TISIPHONE · *the blood avenger*
ALECTO · *the unceasing*

The Erinyes are often represented in graphical form as winged goddesses with serpent hair, and eyes dripping blood. The Erinyes relentlessly pursued their victims until the guilty died in a furore of madness and remorse. So devastating was the power of the Erinyes that the Ancient Greeks dared not speak their real name for fear of provoking their wrath; instead they employed the euphemistic term Eumenides: the kindly ones.

BOXING WEIGHT LIMITS

Fighting class	limit (lbs)
Straw weight	105
Junior Flyweight	108
Flyweight	112
Junior Bantamweight	115
Bantamweight	118
Junior Featherweight	122
Featherweight	126
Junior Lightweight	130
Lightweight	135
Junior Welterweight	140
Welterweight	147
Junior Middleweight	154
Middleweight	160
Super Middleweight	168
Light Heavyweight	175
Cruiserweight	190
Heavyweight	unlimited

DROUGHT

UK METEOROLOGICAL DEFINITIONS

absolute   15 or more consecutive days with rainfall or snow ≤ 0.2mm
partial   29 consecutive days with an average rainfall ≤ 0.2mm per day

Pi

3.141592653589793238462643383279502884197169399375105
8209749445923078164062862089986280348253421170679821
4808651328230664709384460955058223172535940812848111
74502841027019385211055596446229489549303819644288109756
6593344612847564823378678316527120190914564856692346 0348
6104543266482133936072602491412737245870066063155881 7488
15209209628292540917153643678925903600113305305488204665
21384146951941511609433057270365759591953092186117381932
61179310511854807446237996274956735188575272489122793818
30119491298336733624406566430860213949463952247371907021
79860943702770539217176293176752384674818467669405132000
56812714526356082778577134275778960917363717872146844090
12249534301465495853710507922796892589235420199561121290
21960864034418159813629774771309960518707211349999998372
97804995105973173281609631859502445945534690830264252230
82533446850352619311881710100031378387528865875332083814
20617177669147303598253490428755468731159562863882353787
59375195778185778053217122680661300192787661119590921642
01989380952572010654858632788659361533818279682303019520
35301852968995773622599413891249072177528347913151574857
24245415069595082953311686172785588907509838175463746493
93192550604009277016711390098488240128583616035637076601
04710181942955596198946767837449448255379774726847104047

———————————— CAPITAL CITIES ————————————

Andorra	Andorra la Vella	Lesotho	Maseru
Angola	Luanda	Liberia	Monrovia
Armenia	Yerevan	Liechtenstein	Vaduz
Azerbaijan	Baku	Lithuania	Vilnius
Bahamas	Nassau	Macedonia	Skopje
Bahrain	Manama	Madagascar	Antananarivo
Bangladesh	Dhaka	Malawi	Lilongwe
Barbados	Bridgetown	Maldives	Male
Belarus	Minsk	Mali	Bamako
Belize	Belmopan	Marshall Islands	Majuro
Benin	Porto-Novo	Mauritania	Nouakchott
Bhutan	Thimphu	Mauritius	Port Louis
Botswana	Gaborone	Moldova	Chisinau
Brazil	Brasília	Mongolia	Ulaanbaatar
Bulgaria	Sofia	Mozambique	Maputo
Burkina Faso	Ouagadougou	Namibia	Windhoek
Burundi	Bujumbura	Nauru	Yaren District
Cambodia	Phnom Penh	Niger	Niamey
Cape Verde	Praia	Palau[†]	Koror
Chad	N'Djamena	Panama	Panama City
Comoros	Moroni	Paraguay	Asunción
Costa Rica	San José	Portugal	Lisbon
Djibouti	Djibouti	Qatar	Doha
Dominica	Roseau	Rwanda	Kigali
Ecuador	Quito	Samoa	Apia
Equatorial Guinea	Malabo	San Marino	San Marino
Eritrea	Asmara	Saudi Arabia	Riyadh
Gabon	Libreville	Senegal	Dakar
Georgia	T'bilisi	Seychelles	Victoria
Grenada	Saint George's	Sierra Leone	Freetown
Guatemala	Guatemala City	Solomon Islands	Honiara
Guinea	Conakry	Somalia	Mogadishu
Guinea-Bissau	Bissau	Sudan	Khartoum
Guyana	Georgetown	Surinam	Paramaribo
Haiti	Port-au-Prince	Togo	Lomé
Holy See	Vatican City	Tonga	Nuku'alofa
Honduras	Tegucigalpa	Turkmenistan	Ashgabat
Indonesia	Jakarta	Tuvalu	Funafuti Atoll
Kazakhstan	Astana	Uzbekistan	Tashkent
Kiribati	Tarawa	Vanuatu	Port-Vila
Kyrgyzstan	Bishkek	Zambia	Lusaka
Laos	Vientiane		
Latvia	Riga		

† *A new capital for Palau is currently
under construction in Eastern Babelthuap.*

POLYGONS

3 sides	triangle	11	undecagon
4	quadrilateral	12	dodecagon
5	pentagon	13	tridecagon
6	hexagon	14	quadridecagon
7	heptagon	15	pentadecagon
8	octagon	16	hexadecagon
9	nonagon/enneagon	17	heptadecagon
10	decagon	18	octadecagon

ELECTRICAL & TV DATA

Country	Voltage	Frequency	TV Standard
Australia	240V	50Hz	PAL
Austria	230V	50Hz	PAL
Belgium	230V	50Hz	PAL
Brazil	110/127/220V	60Hz	PAL
Canada	120/240V	60Hz	NTSC
China	220V	50Hz	PAL
France	230V	50Hz	SECAM
Germany	230V	50Hz	PAL
Hong Kong	200/220V	50Hz	PAL
Ireland	230V	50Hz	PAL
Israel	230V	50Hz	PAL
Italy	220V	50Hz	PAL
Jamaica	110/220V	50Hz	NTSC
Jordan	230V	50Hz	PAL
South Africa	220/230V	50Hz	PAL
Spain	230V	50Hz	PAL
Switzerland	230V	50Hz	PAL
USA	120/240V	60Hz	NTSC

Voltages may vary & some states are changing voltages. Seek advice before using equipment.

SOUND LEVELS – DECIBELS

0 db	Inaudible	90	City traffic, very annoying
10	Just audible	100	Firecrackers
30	Soft whisper (15ft)	110	Rock concert, power saw
40	Quiet office, living room		*– danger of permanent damage –*
60	Conversational speech	120	Car horn (3ft)
70	Noisy restaurant, intrusive	140	Air-raid siren, jet take-off
80	Hair-dryer, annoying	150	Rocket launch pad

CHAT ROOM ACRONYMS

LOVE & LUST

WTGP? . . . . want to go private?
BF / GF . . . . boy (girl) friend
H&K . . . . hugs and kisses
IWALU . . . . . . I will always love you
DIKU? . . . . do I know you?
HAGN . . . . have a good night
ILY . . . . I love you
LJBF . . . . let's just be friends
SYT . . . . sweet young thing
FOAF . . . . friend of a friend
A/S/L? . . . . age/sex/location?
KOL . . . . kiss on lips
SO . . . . significant other
LY4E . . . . love you forever
SUAKM . . . . shut up and kiss me

TECHNICAL

RTBM . . . . . read the bloody manual
RTM . . . . read the manual
RYS . . . . read your screen
FAQ . . . . frequently asked questions
BRS . . . . big red switch
IRL . . . . in real life
MOTD . . . . message of the day
TPTB . . . . the powers that be
SLM . . . . see last mail
PDS . . . . please don't shout
TSR . . . . totally stupid rules
RHIP . . . . rank has its privileges

LAUGHING & CRYING

CSG . . . . chuckle, snicker, grin
LOL . . . . laughing out loud
BWL . . . . bursting with laughter
LMAO . . . . laughing my ass off
CID . . . . crying in disgrace
CRBT . . . . crying real big tears
SWL . . . . . . screaming with laughter
BEG . . . . big evil grin
ROFL . . . . rolling on floor laughing
JK . . . . just kidding
SICS . . . . sitting in chair snickering

ARGUMENTATIVE

BION . . . . believe it or not
AAMOF . . . . as a matter of fact
BOT . . . . back on topic
$0.02 . . . . my two cents
AFAIK . . . . as far as I know
PMBI . . . . pardon my butting in
IAAA . . . . I am an accountant
IAAL . . . . I am a lawyer
INPO . . . . in no particular order
FCOL . . . . for crying out loud
IOW . . . . in other words
GMTA . . . . . great minds think alike
OAUS . . . . . on an unrelated subject
IJWTS . . . . I just want to say
IMHO . . . . . in my humble opinion
IANALB . . . . I am not a lawyer, but
OTOH . . . . on the other hand
ITFA . . . . in the final analysis
PTMM . . . . please tell me more

MISCELLANEOUS

KISS . . . . keep it simple, stupid
AFK . . . . away from keyboard
NRN . . . . no reply necessary
FUD . . . . fear, uncertainty & doubt
12345 . . . . talk about school
BRB . . . . be right back
F2F . . . . face to face
BTW . . . . by the way
NQA . . . . no questions asked
YMMV . . . . . your mileage may vary
TANJ . . . . there ain't no justice
POV . . . . point of view
L8R G8R . . . . later 'gator
HTH . . . . hope that helps!
YGLT . . . . you're gonna love this
TYCLO . . . . turn your caps lock off!
LTNT . . . . long time, no type
SWIM . . . . see what I mean?
WAEF . . . . when all else fails
TOBAL . . . . . . there oughta be a law
NBD . . . . no big deal

ASTRONOMERS ROYAL

Rev. John Flamsteed	1675	Sir Frank Dyson	1910
Dr Edmond Halley	1720	Sir Harold Spencer Jones	1933
Rev. James Bradley	1742	Sir Richard van der Riet Woolley	
Rev. Nathaniel Bliss	1762		1956
Rev. Nevil Maskelyne	1765	Prof. Sir Martin Ryle	1972
John Pond	1811	Prof. Sir Francis Smith	1982
Sir George Airy	1835	Prof. Sir Arnold Wolfendale	1991
Sir William Christie	1881	Prof. Sir Martin Rees	1995

The Royal Greenwich Observatory was founded by Royal Decree of Charles II in 1675. At its head was the first Astronomer Royal, Rev. John Flamsteed, who was ordered by the King:

'...to apply himself with the most exact care and diligence to the rectifying of the tables of the motions of the heavens, and the places of the fixed stars, so as to find out the so much desired longitude of places for the perfecting the art of navigation.'

SOME SHAKESPEAREAN INSULTS

You are not worth another word, else I'd call you Knave.

Why art thou then exasperate, thou idle immaterial skein of sleave-silk, thou green sarsenet flap for a sore eye, thou tassel of a prodigal's purse, thou? Ah, how the world is pestered with such waterflies, diminutives of nature.

Thou whoreson zed, thou unnecessary letter.

This woman's an easy glove, my Lord, she goes off and on at pleasure.

False of Heart, light of Ear, bloody handed, Hog in sloth, Fox in stealth, Wolf in greediness, Dog in madness, Lion in prey.

You shew'd your teethes like Apes, and fawn'd like hounds and bow'd like Bondmen.

Like the toad, ugly and venomous.

I would thou didst itch from head to foot and I had the scratching of thee; I would make thee the loathsomest scab in Greece.

You fat and greazy citizens.

Like a villaine with a smiling cheek, a goodly apple rotten at the heart.

You common cry of curs! whose breath I hate as reek o' th' rotten fens, whose loves I prize as the dead carcasses of unburied men that do corrupt my air.

DECLARED NUCLEAR POWERS

United States of America · Russia · China
United Kingdom · France · Pakistan · India · [Israel]

COMMONLY 'MISSPELED' WORDS

absence	diarrhoea	mischievous	salary
accessible	disappearance	misspelled	separate
accidentally	drunkenness	mysterious	shining
acclaim	embarrass	necessary	skiing
aggravate	entrepreneur	obsolescent	soliloquy
alleged	existence	omelette	stubbornness
auxiliary	exuberance	origin	subtlety
basically	fascinate	parallel	success
because	fictitious	pastime	suddenness
beginning	forfeit	perseverance	surreptitious
believe	fulfilment	presumptuous	temperamental
biscuit	guarantee	pseudonym	tendency
broccoli	hindrance	pursue	tomorrow
business	idiosyncrasy	realistically	transferred
calendar	immediately	receive	truly
collectible	independent	recommend	twelfth
commitment	indispensable	remembrance	tyranny
connoisseur	inevitable	restaurant	unnecessary
conscientious	intelligence	rhythmical	until
consciousness	interesting	roommate	usage
corroborate	mediocre	sacrilegious	vacuum

LETTER TRAITS

No curved lines	A·E·F·H·I·K·L·M·N·T·V·W·X·Z
No straight lines	C·O·S
No enclosed areas	C·E·F·G·I·J·K·L·M·N·S·T·U·V·W·X·Y·Z
Horizontal symmetry	B·C·D·E·H·I·K·O·X·
Vertical symmetry	A·H·I·M·O·T·U·V·W·X·Y
Roman numerals	C·D·I·L·M·V·X
Just dots in Morse Code	E·H·I·S
Just dashes in Morse Code	M·O·T
Horizontal and vertical symmetry	H·I·O·X
Look the same upside down	H·I·N·O·S·X·Z
Can be drawn in one stroke	B·C·D·G·I·J·L·M·N·O·P·R·S·U·V·W·Z
Capitals which look like lowercase	C·O·P·S·U·V·W·X·Z

YIDDISH

Billik.. cheap, poor quality
Bobkes.. worthless trifles
Bubbee... term of endearment
Chutzpah.. nerve, brazenness, cheek
Danken Got! .... thank God!
Drek... junk, rubbish
Frum .... religiously devout
Gai avek! .... go away
Gelt.. money
Goy .... a non-Jew, gentile
Kaddish .... a prayer in mourning
Kibbitzer... interfering person
Klutz, Klotz.. a clumsy person
K'vetsh .... to whine or complain
Le'chayim!.................................... the traditional toast 'to life'
Loch in kop .... hole in the head
Mashugga, Meshughe...................................... crazy, bonkers
Mazel Tov .... congratulations, good luck!
Mieskeit.. an ugly person or thing
Mitzveh.............................. a good deed, a commandment
Naches .... pride, joy [often that occasioned by children]
Nebbish...................... a nobody, a weakling or awkward person
Nosh .... snack food; to snack
Nu? .... so?
Nudnick...................... a pest, a bore; often a term of endearment
Oi! .... all-purpose exclamation
Oi, gevald! .... exclamation of torment
Schmuck, Shmock .... dick
Shaitel........................... wig worn by Orthodox married women
Shalom .... peace, a greeting
Shikseh .... non-Jewish girl
Shlep (or Shlap)..................................... to carry unwillingly
Shmaltzy .... sentimental, sickly, corny
Shmendrik .... a foolish, inept person
Shmoe.............................. a naïve, easily deceived individual
Shmuts .... dirt, mess
Shmutter, Shmatter .... stuff, clutter, or a general term for cloth
Shnorrer.. a beggar
Shtik .... a special (theatrical) trick or turn
Shul....................................... informal term for synagogue
Toches .... arse
Traif .... forbidden (non-kosher) food
Tsores .... woe, troubles

BOATSWAIN'S CALLS

The Boatswain's Call is the traditional method of issuing certain orders on naval vessels. The orders are known as 'Pipes'; each pipe has its own sound and meaning. The pipe itself is capable of making a high and low note, as well as various trills and warbles.

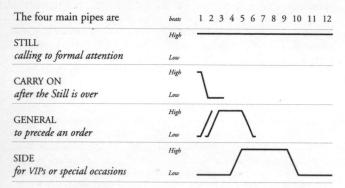

Very few people are honoured by being piped 'the Side', they include: HM the Queen, members of the Royal Family (when in uniform), Royal Navy officers of Flag Rank, and foreign naval officers. The Side is also piped during the formal ceremony when a body is committed to the sea.

LLANFAIR PG · 53°13′N 4°12′W

The longest place name in Britain is said to be that of Anglesey village
Llanfairpwllgwyngyllgogerychwyrndrobwllllantysiliogogogoch (58 letters)
which translates as 'The church of St Mary in a hollow of white hazel
near a rapid whirlpool and near St Tysilio's church by the red cave'.
The name was invented in the nineteenth century as a lure to tourists.

ANIMAL AGES

According to Celtic legend

Thrice the age of a dog is that of a horse;
Thrice the age of a horse is that of a man;
Thrice the age of a man is that of a deer;
Thrice the age of a deer is that of an eagle.

———————— THE IRISH CODE DUELLO ————————

In 1777, during the Clonmell Summer Assizes, the Gentlemen delegates of Tipperary, Galway, Mayo, Sligo, and Roscommon prescribed a series of rules governing the practice of duelling and settling points of honour. It was recommended that 'Gentlemen throughout the Kingdom' should keep a copy in their pistol cases, 'that ignorance might never be pleaded'.

1. The first offence requires the first apology, though the retort may have been more offensive than the insult.

4. When the *lie direct* is the *first* offence, the aggressor must either beg pardon in express terms, exchange two shots previous to apology, or three shots followed up by explanation; or fire on until a severe hit be received by one party or the other.

5. As a blow is strictly prohibited under any circumstances among Gentlemen, no verbal apology can be received for such an insult.

7. But no apology can be received, in any case, after the parties have actually taken their ground, without exchange of fires.

10. Any insult to a lady under a Gentleman's care or protection to be considered as, by one degree, a greater offence than if given to the gentleman personally, and to be regulated accordingly.

14. Seconds to be of equal rank in society with the principals they attend, inasmuch as a second may either choose or chance to become a principal, and *equality is indispensable*.

15. Challenges are never to be delivered at night, unless the party to be challenged intend leaving the place of offence before morning; for it is desirable to avoid all hot-headed proceedings.

16. The challenged has the right to choose his own weapon, unless the challenger gives his honour he is no swordsman; after which, however, he cannot decline any *second* species of weapon proposed by the challenger.

17. The challenged chooses his ground; the challenger chooses his distance; the seconds fix the time and terms of firing.

21. Seconds are bound to attempt a reconciliation *before* the meeting takes place, or *after* sufficient firing or hits, as specified.

22. Any wound sufficient to agitate the nerves and necessarily make the hand shake, must end the business for *that day*.

25. Where seconds disagree, and resolve to exchange shots themselves, it must be at the same time and at right angles with their principals. If with swords, side by side, with five paces interval.

ENGLISH MONARCHS

Danish Line

Svein Forkbeard.............. 1014
Canute the Great.......... 1017–35
Harald Harefoot........... 1035–40
Hardicanute............... 1040–42
Edward the Confessor..... 1042–66
Harold II.................. 1066

Norman Line

William the Conqueror ... 1066–87
William II Rufus 1087–1100
Henry I Beauclerc 1100–35
Stephen.................... 1135–54
Henry II Curtmantle 1154–89
Richard I the Lionheart ... 1189–99
John...................... 1199–1216
Henry III 1216–72
Edward I 1272–1307
Edward II................. 1307–27
Edward III 1327–77
Richard II................. 1377–99

Plantagenet, Lancastrian Line

Henry IV 1399–1413
Henry V 1413–22
Henry VI 1422–61, 1470–71

Plantagenet, Yorkist Line

Edward IV 1461–70, 1471–83
Edward V 1483
Richard III Crookback..... 1483–85

House of Tudor

Henry VII Tudor 1485–1509
Henry VIII................. 1509–47
Edward VI 1547–53
Lady Jane Grey......... [9 days] 1553
Mary I Tudor 1553–8
Elizabeth I............... 1558–1603

House of Stuart

James I..................... 1603–25
Charles I.................. 1625–49

Commonwealth

Oliver Cromwell 1649–58
Richard Cromwell........ 1658–59

House of Stuart, Restored

Charles II 1660–85
James II.................... 1685–88

House of Orange and Stuart

William III, Mary II 1689–1702

House of Stuart

Anne....................... 1702–14

House of Brunswick, Hanover

George I 1714–27
George II 1727–60
George III 1760–1820
George IV................... 1820–30
William IV................. 1830–37
Victoria.................. 1837–1901

House of Saxe-Coburg-Gotha

Edward VII 1901–10

House of Windsor

George V 1910–36
Edward VIII................... 1936
George VI.................. 1936–52
Elizabeth II 1952–present

MONARCH MNEMONIC

*Willy, Willy, Harry, Stee, Harry, Dick, John,
Harry III. I, II, III Neds, Richard II, Harrys
IV, V, VI... then who? Edwards IV, V, Dick
the bad, Harrys (twain) and Ned the Lad,
Mary, Bessie, James the vain, Charlie,
Charlie, James again... William & Mary,
Anne Gloria, Four Georges, William &
Victoria; Edward VII next & then George V
in 1910; Edward VIII soon abdicated:
George the VI was coronated; After which
Elizabeth, and that's the end until her death.*

PREFIXES

10^{24}	yotta	Y	1 000 000 000 000 000 000 000 000
10^{21}	zetta	Z	1 000 000 000 000 000 000 000
10^{18}	exa	E	1 000 000 000 000 000 000
10^{15}	peta	P	1 000 000 000 000 000
10^{12}	tera	T	1 000 000 000 000
10^{9}	giga	G	1 000 000 000
10^{6}	mega	M	1 000 000
10^{3}	kilo	k	1 000
10^{2}	hecto	h	100
10	deca	da	10
1			1
10^{-1}	deci	d	0.1
10^{-2}	centi	c	0.01
10^{-3}	milli	m	0.001
10^{-6}	micro	u	0.000 001
10^{-9}	nano	n	0.000 000 001
10^{-12}	pico	p	0.000 000 000 001
10^{-13}	femto	f	0.000 000 000 000 001
10^{-18}	atto	a	0.000 000 000 000 000 001
10^{-21}	zepto	z	0.000 000 000 000 000 000 001
10^{-24}	yocto	y	0.000 000 000 000 000 000 000 001

TWELVE LABOURS OF HERCULES

Killing the Nemean Lion
Killing the Hydra of Lerna
Capture of the Ceryneian Hind
Capture of the Erymanthian Boar
Cleaning the Stables of Augeas
Killing the Stymphalian Birds
Capturing the Cretan Bull
Killing the Mares of Diomedes
Acquisition of the Girdle of Hippolyte
Capture of the Cattle of Geryon
Acquisition of the Golden Apples of the Hesperides
Capture of Cerberus in the Underworld

REINDEER

Dasher · Dancer · Prancer · Vixen · Comet
Cupid · Donner · Blitzen · [Rudolph]

POETS LAUREATE

The post of Poet Laureate probably dates back to the reign of Charles II, although prior to that poets, including Ben Jonson, were afforded royal patronage. Though nowadays the post has no formal obligations, most Laureates write on subjects of national interest, concern, and celebration.

1668–1688............John Dryden	1850–1892[‡] . Alfred, Lord Tennyson
1689–1692......Thomas Shadwell	1896–1913 ....Alfred Austin
1692–1715 ....Nahum Tate	1913–1930..........Robert Bridges
1715–1718..........Nicholas Rowe	1930–1967..........John Masefield
1718–1730.......Laurence Eusden	1968–1972 ....Cecil Day Lewis
1730–1757...........Colley Cibber	1972–1984 ......Sir John Betjeman
1757–1785[†] ....William Whitehead	1984–1998.............Ted Hughes
1785–1790 ....Thomas Warton	1998–.............Andrew Motion
1790–1813[§]......Henry James Pye	
1813–1843 ....Robert Southey	Laureate declined by: † Thomas Gray
1843–1850 ...William Wordsworth	§ Walter Scott · ‡ Samuel Rogers

THE TEN COMMANDMENTS

[1] Thou shalt have no other Gods. [2] Thou shalt not make any graven images. [3] Thou shalt not take the Lord's name in vain. [4] Remember the Sabbath day. [5] Honour thy father and mother. [6] Thou shalt not kill. [7] Thou shalt not commit adultery. [8] Thou shalt not steal. [9] Thou shalt not bear false witness against thy neighbour. [10] Thou shalt not covet thy neighbour's house ... nor anything that is his.

TV STANDARDS

NTSC · *National Television System Committee*...........525 Lines/60Hz
PAL · *Phase Alternating Line*.............................625 Lines/50Hz
SECAM · *Sequential Couleur Avec Mémoire*.............625 Lines/50Hz

US PRESIDENTIAL INAUGURATION

On the occasion of an inauguration, with their right hand raised aloft, and their left hand placed on an open Bible, the new President proclaims:

I do solemnly swear [or affirm] *that I will faithfully execute the office of President of the United States, and will, to the best of my ability, preserve, protect, and defend the Constitution of the United States.*

CRICKET FIELDING POSITIONS

z

x

y

w
w
w c
w b
v a

bat

s d
t e
f k l

r

u g h

q i

bowler j

o m

p n

KEY TO POSITIONS	i . . . . mid wicket	r . . . . cover
a . . . . wicket keeper	j . . . . . deep mid wicket	s . . . . point
b . . . . leg slip	k . . . . square leg	t . . . . silly point
c . . . . leg gully	l . . . . . deep square leg	u . . . . silly mid off
d . . . . short square leg	m . . . . mid on	v . . . . gully
e . . . . short leg	n . . . . long on	w . . . . slips (first–third)
f . . . . forward short leg	o . . . . mid off	x . . . . third man
g . . . . silly mid on	p . . . . long off	y . . . . fine leg
h . . . . short mid wicket	q . . . . extra cover	z . . . . deep fine leg

[Obviously, this layout assumes that the batsman is right-handed.]

—————————— EURO NOTE SPECIFICATIONS ——————————

EUROS	COLOUR	ARCHITECTURE	SIZE (MM)
5	Grey	Classical	120 x 62
10	Red	Romanesque	127 x 67
20	Blue	Gothic	133 x 72
50	Orange	Renaissance	140 x 77
100	Green	Rococo & Baroque	147 x 82
200	Brown	Iron & Glass	153 x 82
500	Purple	Modern	160 x 82

—— COLOURS OF THE EMPIRE STATE BUILDING ——

New York's Empire State Building has a complex lighting system which allows the building to be coloured in a variety of combinations. The lights are used to mark national holidays, charitable causes, ethnic celebrations, and the changes of season. The list below shows some of the colour sequences and what they represent: *[Colour sequence is from street level upwards]*

Red, Black, Green	Dr Martin Luther King, Jr. Day
Green	St Patrick's Day, March of Dimes, Earth Day
Red	St Valentine's Day, Fire Department Memorial Day
Red, Blue	Equal Parents Day, Children's Rights
Yellow, White	Spring, Easter Week
Blue, White, Blue	Israel Independence Day, Chanukah First Night
Blue	Police Memorial Day, Child-Abuse Prevention
Purple, White	Alzheimer's Awareness
Red, Yellow, Green	Portugal Day
Red, White, Blue	Flag Day, Presidents' Day, Armed Forces Day Memorial Day, Independence Day, Labor Day, Veterans' Day
Lavender, White	Stonewall Anniversary, Gay Pride
Purple, Teal, White	National Osteoporosis Society
Red, White, Green	Columbus Day
Blue, White	Greek Independence Day, United Nations Day
Black, Yellow, Red	German Reunification Day
Pink & White	Breast-Cancer Awareness
Red, Green	Holiday Season
No Lights	AIDS Awareness

On 4 June 2002, in a rare tribute to a foreign national, the Empire State Building was lit with the unique combination of Royal Purple and Gold to commemorate the Golden Jubilee of HM Queen Elizabeth II. Prior to this, the last non-American to be honoured in light was Nelson Mandela.

EPONYMOUS FOODS

BEEF WELLINGTON *fillet steak wrapped in puff pastry* named to honour the Duke of Wellington.

PAVLOVA *meringue cake* named in honour of the acclaimed ballerina Anna Pavlova.

SAVARIN *rum-flavoured fruit sponge* created by French chef, Antoine Brillat-Savarin.

EARL GREY *China tea infused with bergamot oil* favoured and then popularised by Earl Grey.

FRANGIPANI *almond-flavoured cream* created by Marquis Muzio Frangipani.

APPLE CHARLOTTE *layered apple cake* named after Queen Charlotte, wife of George III.

SALLY LUNN *teacake* said to be created by Sally Lunn, a Bath pastry chef.

MOZARTKUGELN *marzipan with nougat cream, dipped in chocolate* created in Vienna in 1890 by Salzburg confectioner Paul Furst, and named in honour of Mozart.

GARIBALDI BISCUIT *'squashed-fly biscuits'* said to be named after Giuseppe Garibaldi, the Italian Nationalist, who liked them.

MADELEINE *light sponge cake* associated with Madeleine Palmier, a French pastry chef.

SACHERTORTE *rich layered chocolate cake* invented in Vienna by Franz Sacher.

PEACH MELBA *ice cream, peaches, and raspberry sauce* named after soprano Dame Nellie Melba, by Escoffier.

MELBA TOAST *toasted bread, sliced and baked* created at The Ritz to ameliorate Dame Nellie's diet.

THE SANDWICH named after the 11th Earl of Sandwich to facilitate simultaneous eating & gambling.

CHATEAUBRIAND *a deep cut of beef fillet* named after Ambassador Vicomte de Chateaubriand.

LADY GREY *Blended tea with orange & lemon peel, and bergamot oil* named after Lady Grey.

ENVELOPE SIZES

Code	Size [mm]	Fits
C6	114 x 162	A6, A5 ½ folded
DL	110 x 220	A4 ⅓ folded
C6/5	114 x 229	A4 ⅓ folded
C5	162 x 229	A5, A4 ½ folded
C4	229 x 324	A4
C3	324 x 458	A3
B6	125 x 176	C6 envelope
B5	176 x 250	C5 envelope
B4	250 x 353	C4 envelope
E4	280 x 400	B4 envelope

BED SIZES

		IMPERIAL	METRIC cm
UK	(Small) Single	2'6" x 6'3"	75 x 190
	King (Standard) Single	3' x 6'3"	90 x 190
	Three Quarter	4' x 6'3"	120 x 190
	Double	4'6" x 6'3"	135 x 190
	King	5' x 6'3"	153 x 190
	Super King	6' x 6'6"	183 x 200
US	Twin/Single	3'3" x 6'3"	100 x 190
	Twin/Single extra long	3'3" x 6'8"	100 x 203
	Double/Full	4'6" x 6'3"	135 x 190
	Queen	5' x 6'8"	153 x 203
	King	6'6" x 6'8"	200 x 203
	California King	6' x 7'	183 x 213

Many versions of bed size exist; the above is an approximate guide only.

COMPOUND PLURALS

adjutants-general
aides-de-camp
ambassadors at large
attorneys at law
attorneys-general
billets-doux
bills of fare
bodies politic
brothers-in-law
changes of fortune
Chapels Royal
chargés d'affaires
chiefs of staff
coats of arms
commanders-in-chief
comptrollers-general
consuls-general

courts-martial
crêpes suzette
culs-de-sac
cupsful
daddies-long-legs
daughters-in-law
Doctors Who
editors-in-chief
filets mignons
fleurs-de-lis
gins and tonic
governors-general
grants-in-aid
heirs apparent
inspectors-general
knickerbockers glory
listeners-in

men-of-war
ministers-designate
mothers-in-law
passersby
pilots-in-command
Poets Laureate
postmasters-general
presidents-elect
prisoners of war
reductions in force
rights of way
secretaries-general
sergeants-at-arms
sergeants-major
solicitors-general
surgeons-general
trades union

WIVES OF HENRY VIII

Catherine of Aragon · Anne Boleyn · Jane Seymour
Anne of Cleves · Catherine Howard · Catherine Parr
[divorced, beheaded, died, divorced, beheaded, survived]

TUGS OF WAR

Specifications of competition-grade rope, as prescribed by
The Tug of War International Federation:

'The rope must not be less than 10 centimetres (100 mm), or more than 12.5 centimetres (125 mm) in circumference, and must be free from knots or other holdings for the hands. The ends of the rope shall have a whipping finish. The minimum length of the rope must not be less than 33.5 metres.'

HOW TO WRAP A SARI

THE NOBLE GASES

Once thought inert, the Noble Gases are six highly stable monoatomic gaseous elements which constitute Group 0 of the Periodic Table.

Helium (He) · Neon (Ne) · Argon (Ar)
Krypton (Kr) · Xenon (Xe) · Radon (Rn)

All of the Noble Gases were discovered by Sir William Ramsey, except for Radon which was discovered by Fredrich Ernst Dorn.

---------- RECORD SALES ----------

SINGLES		ALBUMS
British Phonographic Industry		
200,000	Silver	60,000
400,000	Gold	100,000
600,000	Platinum	300,000

Recording Industry Association of America

500,000	Gold	500,000
1,000,000	Platinum	1,000,000
10,000,000	Diamond	10,000,000

------- FRENCH REVOLUTIONARY CALENDAR -------

The Revolutionary Calendar was imposed on France by law of 5 October 1793. Dates were calculated from the Autumn Equinox, 22 September 1792, which became the first day of Year 1. The standard year was split into 12 thirty-day months with 5 (or 6) additional days (depending on leap years). The thirty-day months were named by the distinguished poet Fabre d'Eglantine, each with its own appropriate symbolism:

Vendémiaire	vintage	Germinal	seed, budding
Brumaire	fog, mist	Floréal	blossom
Frimaire	frost	Prairial	meadow
Nivôse	snow	Messidor	harvest
Pluviôse	rain	Thermidor	heat
Ventôse	wind	Fructidor	fruits

Each of these months was subdivided into three *décades* of ten days: Pimidi, Duodi, Tridi, Quartidi, Quintidi, Sextidi, Septidi, Octidi, Nonidi and Decadi, the day of rest. The remaining '*sans culottides*' were called:

jour de la vertu	*virtue day*
jour du génie	*genius day*
jour du labour	*labour day*
jour de la raison	*reason day*
jour de la récompense	*reward day*
jour de la révolution	*revolution day* [leap years]

For obvious reasons, the calendar was unwieldy, impractical, and unpopular. Reforms were proposed, but instead Napoleon ordered the re-introduction of the traditional Gregorian Calendar on 1 January 1806, thus condemning the Revolutionary calendar to death on 10 Nivôse XIV.

LATIN ABBREVS

AD	*Anno Domini*	in the year of our Lord
ad lib.	*ad libitum*	as much as you like
ad loc.	*ad locum*	indicating the place referred to
a.m.	*ante meridiem*	before noon
AMDG	*Ad Majorem Dei Gloriam*	to the greater glory of God
ca. or c.	*circa*	around
cf.	*confer*	compare with
DV	*Deo volente*	God willing
et al.	*et alii*	and other things
etc.	*etcetera*	and so on
fl.	*floruit*	the zenith of a person's life
ibid.	*ibidem*	in the same source
i.e.	*id est*	that is
loc. cit.	*loco citato*	in the place previously cited
MA	*Magister Artium*	master of arts
MD	*Medicinae Doctor*	doctor of medicine
MO	*modus operandi*	method of operating
NB	*nota bene*	note well
nem. con.	*nemine contradicente*	unanimously
non seq.	*non sequitur*	it does not follow
op.	*opus*	piece of work
op. cit.	*opere citato*	in the work already mentioned
p.a.	*per annum*	each year
p.m.	*post meridiem*	afternoon
pp	*per pro*	on behalf of
pro tem.	*pro tempore*	for the time, temporarily
p.s.	*post scriptum*	written after
q.e.d.	*quod erat demonstrandum*	thus proved
q.v.	*quod vide*	referring to text within a work
RIP	*requiescat in pace*	may he rest in peace
sic	*sic*	thus, or literally
v.	*vide*	see, look up
v. inf.	*vide infra*	see below
viz	*videlicet*	that is to say, namely
vox pop.	*vox populi*	voice of the people
vs.	*versus*	against

OPEC MEMBERS

Organisation of the Petroleum Exporting Countries
Algeria · Indonesia · Iran · Iraq · Kuwait · Libya · Nigeria · Qatar
Saudi Arabia · United Arab Emirates · Venezuela

THE FLAG OF KIRIBATI

The top half is red, with a yellow frigate bird flying (right to left) over a rising sun. The bottom half is dark blue with white waves forming a sea.

EGG SIZES

TRADITIONAL SIZES

Size 0	>75g	Size 4	55g – 60g
Size 1	70g – 75g	Size 5	50g – 55g
Size 2	65g – 70g	Size 6	45g – 50g
Size 3	60g – 65g	Size 7	<45g

MODERN SIZES

Very Large (XL)	>73g	Medium (M)	53g – 63g
Large (L)	63g – 73g	Small (S)	<53g

VICTORIAN TIMETABLE OF FAMILY MOURNING

After the death of her beloved Albert in 1861, Queen Victoria set the standard for mourning. Befitting the age, outward displays were key: grief was represented on many levels, from the use of black-lined stationery and jet-black jewellery, to elaborate funeral arrangements, and periods of self-imposed social exile. Curiously, the period of mourning was decided not by personal sentiment but by a socially understood timetable of grief:

Death of	Period of mourning		
Husband	two to three years	Grandparents	six months
Wife	three months	Aunts & Uncles	three months
Parent or Child	one year	Nephews & Nieces	two months
Siblings	six months	Great Uncles & Aunts	six weeks
		First Cousins	four–six weeks

These individual mourning periods were themselves subdivided into first mourning, second mourning, ordinary, and half-mourning. By tradition first mourning was the deepest and lasted a year and a day. Each of these periods had its own subtle code – down to the shade of black, the types of cloth worn, and the width of hat-bands. Older children were expected to mourn alongside their parents, but often very young children were excused mourning dress. Servants' Mourning was normally considered appropriate after the death of a senior member of the household; when imposed, it usually lasted for at least six months. Never one to do things by half, Victoria wore mourning dress for the forty years until her death.

NAVAL TIME KEEPING

The traditional naval watches are based on the following time periods:

Time (24hr)	Watch		
00:00 – 04:00 ...... *Middle Watch*	12:00 – 16:00 .... *Afternoon Watch*
04:00 – 08:00 ..... *Morning Watch*	16:00 – 18:00 .... *First Dog Watch*
08:00 – 12:00 ..... *Forenoon Watch*	18:00 – 20:00 ..... *Last Dog Watch*
	20:00 – 00:00 .... *First Watch*

During the four-hour watches, bells are struck every half-hour in the following order. [To avoid confusion, bells are struck in pairs, with any odd bell struck afterwards: e.g. 5 bells would be *bell-bell / bell-bell / bell*.]

First half-hour .... *1 bell*	Fifth half-hour .... *5 bells*
First hour .... *2 bells*	Third hour .... *6 bells*
Third half-hour .... *3 bells*	Seventh half-hour .... *7 bells*
Second hour .... *4 bells*	Fourth hour .... *8 bells*

At the end of the First Dog Watch (18:00) 4 bells are struck (not the 8 that usually signify a change of watch). The Last Dog Watch bells are:

18:30 .... *1 bell*	19:30 .... *3 bells*
19:00 .... *2 bells*	20:00 .... *8 bells*

By tradition, 16 bells are struck to mark midnight on New Year's Eve.

BRONTË SIBLINGS

Charlotte (1816-55) · Emily (1818-48) · Anne (1820-49) · Branwell (1817-48)

PIG LATIN HAMLET

Otay ebay, orway otnay otay ebay: atthay isway ethay estionquay:
Etherwhay 'istay oblernay inway ethay indmay otay uffersay
Ethay ingsslay andway arrowsway ofway outrageousway ortunefay,
Orway otay aketay armsway againstway away easay ofway oublestray,
Andway ybay opposingway endway emthay?

To be, or not to be: that is the question:
Whether 'tis nobler in the mind to suffer
The slings and arrows of outrageous fortune,
Or to take arms against a sea of troubles,
And by opposing end them?

By tradition, the only British Army regiments that are allowed to march through the City of London with bayonets fixed and Colours flying are:

*3rd Battalion of the Grenadier Guards · 2nd Battalion of the Gloucesters
The Royal Fusiliers (City of London Regiment) · The Buffs*

—— ORCHESTRA SCHEMATIC ——

PERCUSSION · TIMPANI

FRENCH HORNS · TRUMPETS · TROMBONES · TUBAS

CLARINETS · BASSOONS · CONTRA-BASSOONS

PICCOLOS · FLUTES · OBOES · CORS ANGLAIS · DOUBLE BASSES

PIANO · HARP · FIRST VIOLINS · SECOND VIOLINS · VIOLAS · CELLOS

CONDUCTOR

—— TUSSER ON THRIFTINESS ——

Tusser's 1557 poem *Thriftiness*, every word of which begins with a 't':

The thrifty that teacheth the thriving to thrive,
Teach timely to traverse, the thing that thou 'trive,
Transferring thy toiling, to timeliness taught,
This teacheth thee temp'rance, to temper thy thought,
Take Trusty (to trust to) that thinkest to thee,
That trustily thriftiness trowleth to thee.
Then temper thy travell, to tarry the tide;
This teacheth thee thriftiness, twenty times tryed,
Take thankfull thy talent, thank thankfully those
That thriftily teach thee thy time to transpose.
Troth twice to be teached, teach twenty times ten,
This trade thou that takest, take thrift to thee then.

THE OLD CLAUSE IV OF THE
LABOUR PARTY CONSTITUTION

'To secure for the workers by hand or by brain the full fruits of their industry and the most equitable distribution thereof that may be possible upon the basis of the common ownership of the means of production, distribution, and exchange, and the best obtainable system of popular administration and control of each industry or service.'

Clause IV was modified in 1996, when the constitution was re-written.

SOME BALLET TERMS

CAMBRÉ · a bend from the waist.

CHANGEMENT · a jump where the position of the feet is changed.

ENCHAÎNEMENT · a series of steps linked together in a sequence.

ENTRECHAT · a jump where the legs criss-cross in the air.

FOUETTÉ · whipping move of the leg, often to create momentum to perform a turn or jump.

JETÉ · basic ballet step; a jump from one foot to the other.

PAS · a basic ballet step; often omitted as a prefix in ballet terms.

PAS DE DEUX · dance for two.

PAS DE QUATRE · dance for four.

PIROUETTE · a complete turn, or series of turns, on one leg.

PLIÉ · bending of the knees.

RELEVÉ · rising up off the heels.

SAUT · a jump off both feet landing in the same position.

SUR LES POINTES · on points.

TERRE À TERRE · steps where the feet hardly leave the ground.

VARIATION · a solo dance.

CANASTA SCORING

4s, 5s, 6s, 7s, 8s, 9s	5	
10s, Js, Qs, Ks	10	
2s, Aces	20	
Jokers	50	
Black 3s [where allowed]	5	
Red 3s	100	
All 4 Red 3s	800	
Pure Canasta	500	

Impure Canasta	300
Going out	100
Going out concealed	200
MINIMUM MELD VALUE TO GO DOWN	
Negative score	15
Score of 0–1495	50
Score of 1500–2995	90
Score of >3000	120

SOME NAMED HAYDN SYMPHONIES

No.	Key	Name
22	E flat	The Philosopher
43	E flat	Mercury
45	F sharp minor	Farewell
48	C	Maria Theresia
55	E flat	The Schoolmaster
59	A	Fire
82	C	The Bear
83	G minor	The Hen
85	B flat	The Queen
94	G	The Surprise
96	D	The Miracle
100	G	The Military
103	E flat	The Drum Roll

COMMONPLACE GERMAN

Angst .... inner fear or torment, objectless anxiety
Bildungsroman .... novel describing personal development
Echt .... real, genuine, authentic
Ersatz .... substitute, fake, imitation
Festschrift .... a commemorative publication to honour a colleague
Gedankenexperiment .... thought experiment
Gemütlich .... cosy, welcoming, pleasant
Gestalt .... the overall shape or pattern of something
Götterdämmerung .. 'twilight of the Gods'; downfall of the once mighty
Hinterland ...... a private, personal space (usually outside of one's work)
Kaffeeklatsch .... coffee culture, café society
Kitsch .... inauthentic, vulgar, tacky, derivative, or cheap
Leitmotiv .... a recurring theme
Meister .... used as a suffix to mean expert, or master
Realpolitik .... real-life, often cynical, politics
Schadenfreude .... malicious pleasure in the misfortune of others
Schmalz .... sickly sentimentality
Spiel .... a glib, well-rehearsed patter
Sturm und Drang .... Storm and Stress; late 18th-century romantic style
Urtext .... original, authorised text
Verboten .... forbidden, prohibited
Wanderlust .... a yearning to travel
Weltanschauung .... a world view, a philosophy of life
Weltschmerz .... world weariness; despair with the world
Wunderkind .... child prodigy
Zeitgeist .... the spirit of the age

BA RESULTS RHYMING SLANG

I	Geoff (Hurst)	II:II	Desmond (Tutu)
II:I	Attila (The Hun)	III	Douglas (Hurd)

——SOME DEITIES OF VARIOUS CULTURES——

EGYPTIAN

Ra .... sun
Khepera .... rising sun
Nut........... sky, heaven
Geb................. Earth
Hathor .... love, joy
Seth .. night, evil, turmoil
Horus .... light, all-seeing
Min............... fertility
Osiris.... life, underworld
Anubis .... lost, dead
Sekhmet .... wrath, might

JAPANESE

Ama-terasu .... Gods, sun
Kagutschi .... fire
Ebisu........... fisherman
Uzume......... happiness
Susanowa .... thunder
Tsuki-yumi .... moon
Wakahiru-me .. rising sun
Benten .... music, luck
Inari .... rice
Ukemochi ,, food, fertility

NORSE

Odin................ Gods
Thor ...... thunder, crops
Freya ..... passion, beauty
Tyr .... battle, law
Loki .... mischief
Forseti .... justice
Hel .... underworld

HINDU

Brahma........... Creator
Vishnu.......... Preserver
Shiva .... regeneration
Agni .... fire
Krishna .... love
Ganesh ..... wisdom, luck
Indra .... rain, thunder
Lakshmi .. beauty, fortune

GREEK	DEITY OF	ROMAN
Aphrodite .... love.............. Venus
Hephaestus .... fire .... Vulcan
Apollo............. light .... Apollo
Poseidon .... sea.......... Neptune
Ares................. war .... Mars
Hermes ..... travellers, thieves.... Mercury
Artemis ..... hunting, fertility ...... Diana
Hades .... underworld.......... Pluto
Asclepius......... healing .... Aesculapius
Dionysus.......... wine .... Bacchus
Eros............. love, desire......... Cupid
Zeus.......... ruler of Gods .... Jupiter
Nike .... victory .... Victoria
Amphitrite ...... sea, salt .... Salacia
Eurus .... east wind ...... Vulturus
Hestia ,,, hearth, home......... Vesta
Tyche............. fortune .... Fortuna
Pan .... herds .... Faunus
Palaemon ... harbours .... Portunus
Dike .... justice......... Astraea
Persephone ...... spring ...... Proserpina
Helios .... sun .... Sol
Aletheia............ truth............. Veritas
Notus.......... south wind......... Auster
Hebe .... youth........ Juventas
Eos .... dawn .... Aurora
Priapus .... fecundity....... Mutinus
Cronus........... harvest........ Saturnus
Selene .... moon .... Luna
Proteus .... prophecy ...... Carmenta
Boreas .... north wind ... Aquilo
Enyo.............. war.......... Bellona
Eris........ strife, discord .... Discordia
Chloris .... spring............. Flora
Thanatos .... death .... Mors
Thalia .... comedy......... Comus
Athena .... wisdom .... Minerva
Gaea........... the Earth .... Terra
Hera .... marriage............ Juno
Hypnos .... sleep .... Somnus

There are wide variations in spelling. Also, some gods had influence in many spheres, often sharing powers with other deities.

———————— COMMONPLACE LATIN ————————

a posteriori . . . . reasoning or knowledge derived from experience
a priori . . . . reasoning or knowledge derived from first principles
alma mater . . . . nurturing mother [often old school or college]
alter ego . . . . other self; alternative personality
amor patriae . . . . love of country
annus mirabilis . . . . wonderful, remarkable year
apologia pro vita sua . . . . a justification of his life
ars longa, vita brevis . . . . art is long, life is short
casus belli . . . . the grounds of a dispute; an occasion for war
caveat emptor . . . . let the buyer beware
corpus delicti . . . . the evidence or body of a crime
cui bono? . . . . to whom good? who stands to gain?
de facto . . . . in reality; according to practice
de profundis . . . . out of the depths
et nunc et semper . . . . now and forever
ex cathedra . . . . an authoritative pronouncement
ex more . . . . according to custom
ex officio . . . . by virtue of one's office or position
ex post facto . . . . after the deed; retrospectively
flagrante delicto . . . . in the act of a crime
in loco parentis . . . . in place of a parent
in medias res . . . . into the middle of things
in vino veritas . . . . there is truth in wine; truth is spoken with wine
infra dig(nitatem) . . . . below one's dignity; lowering oneself
inter alia . . . . amongst other things
ipso facto . . . . by the fact itself
memento mori . . . . a reminder of death and mortality
mens sana in corpore sano . . . . a healthy mind in a healthy body
mutatis mutandis . . . . with the necessary changes having been made
ne plus ultra . . . . no more beyond; the zenith
(non) compos mentis . . . . (not) of sound mind
obiter dictum . . . . an incidental remark
passim . . . . everywhere, throughout
pax vobiscum . . . . peace be with you
persona non grata . . . . unwelcome, or unacceptable person
primus inter pares . . . . first among equals; often attributed to the PM
pro patria . . . . for one's country
quis custodiet ipsos custodes? . . . . who watches the watchmen?
sine qua non . . . . without which nothing; a prerequisite
sub rosa . . . . communicated in secret
sui generis . . . . of its own kind, unique, a class alone
summa cum laude . . . . with highest praise
ultra vires . . . . beyond its legal authority

──────── THE LANGUAGE OF FLOWERS ────────

English Society learned a formal language of flowers from writers like Aubry de la Mottraye and Lady Mary Wortley Montagu, who brought back complex taxonomies of floral meanings from their travels abroad. Throughout the eighteenth and nineteenth centuries, a whole class of pale and listless ladies was preoccupied with the construction of subtle floral codes for their friends and admirers. A very few examples from these long and complex floral vocabularies are shown below:

Coquetry	Morning Glory	*Dangerous pleasures*	Tuberose
Concealed love	Acacia	*Curiosity*	Sycamore
You are cold	Hortensia	*Disdain*	Rue
Heart's ease	Pansy	*I am worthy of you*	White Rose
Ingratitude	Buttercups	*Perseverance*	Magnolia
Neglected beauty	Throatwood	*Foppery*	Coxcomb

Complementing this vocabulary was a specific grammar of floral arrangement. Flowers arranged on the left signified the sender, whereas those on the right represented the recipient. A flower presented upside-down would have its meaning reversed – so, a pansy set upright would signify 'heart's ease', but inverted would represent 'a distressed heart'. If the thorns of a flower were stripped it signified 'hope', but if the leaves were stripped it signified 'fear'. Numbers were denoted by an even more elaborate system of berries, leaves, and foliage. Thus, if a man wanted to present a subtle declaration of love to a girl on her 19th birthday he might present an evergreen wreath [*lasting as my affection*], with ten leaflets and nine berries [*19 years*], a red rose-bud [*pure and lovely*], ivy [*friendship*], and some peach-blossom [*I am your captive*]. This might then be gilded with periwinkle [*sweet remembrances*], and bachelor's-button [*love's hope*].

──────── SOME EPONYMOUS WORDS ────────

HANSARD (Parliamentary record)	Luke Hansard (1752–1828)
BUNSEN (burner)	Professor R.W. Bunsen (1811–99)
SAM BROWNE (army belt)	General Sir Sam Browne (1811–99)
BRAILLE	Louis Braille (1809–52)
SILHOUETTE	Etienne de Silhouette (1709–67)
BOWDLERIZE (to expurgate)	Thomas Bowdler (1754–1825)
QUISLING (traitor)	Vidkun Quisling (1887–1945)
SADISM	Marquis de Sade (1740–1814)
WELLINGTON (boot)	1st Duke of Wellington (1769–1852)
BOYCOTT	Captain Charles Cunningham Boycott (1832–97)
MANSARD (roof)	François Mansard (1598–1666)

CHURCHILL & RHETORIC

One of the greatest orators of the twentieth century, Winston Churchill understood the power of the tropes of classical rhetoric. The table below gives some rhetorical techniques, and provides Churchillian examples.

LITOTES
Deliberate understatement for dramatic or comic effect.
'Business carried on as usual during alterations on the map of Europe.'

PARADOX
A contradictory, but often revealing, logical anomaly.
'... decided only to be undecided, resolved to be irresolute, adamant for drift, solid for fluidity ...'

PARONOMASIA
Using similar-sounding words or phrases for effect.
'To jaw-jaw is always better than to war-war.'

PERIPHRASIS
Circuitously elaborate expression.
'... it cannot in the opinion of His Majesty's Government be classified as slavery in the extreme acceptance of the word without some risk of terminological inexactitude.'

CATACHRESIS
An unexpected image which stretches normal usage.
'a new Dark Age made more sinister ... by the lights of perverted science.'

EPIZEUXIS
Emphatic repetition.
'... this is the lesson: never give in, never give in, never, never, never, never ...'

EPISTROPHE / ANTISTROPHE
Repetition of words at the end of successive phrases.
'... the love of peace, the toil for peace, the strife for peace, the pursuit of peace ...'

ANTITHESIS
Juxtaposition of contrasting ideas with symmetrical phrasing.
'If we are together nothing is impossible, if we are divided all will fail.'

OXYMORON
The juxtaposition of two contradictory words or images.
'...an iron curtain has descended across the Continent.'

METONYMY
Use of a single term or image to represent a wider concept.
'We welcome Russia to her rightful place ... We welcome her flag upon the seas.'

CACOPHONY
Employment of harsh phrasing.
'that hideous apparatus of aggression which gashed Holland into ruin and slavery ...'

ANTIMETABOLE
Reversing the word order of a phrase previously employed.
'This is not the end. It is not even the beginning of the end. But it is, perhaps, the end of the beginning.'

CHURCHILL & RHETORIC cont.

SCESIS ONOMATON
Emphatic synonymous repetition.
'Our difficulties and danger will not be removed by closing our eyes to them. They will not be removed by mere waiting to see what happens; nor will they be removed by a policy of appeasement.'

ASSONANCE & ALLITERATION
Repetition of vowel [assonance] and consonant [alliteration] sounds.
'Let it roll. Let it roll on full flood, inexorable, irresistible, benignant, to broader lands and better days.'

BRACHYLOGIA
Abbreviated expression.
'That was our constant fear: one blow after another, terrible losses, frightful dangers. Everything miscarried.'

ANAPHORA
Repetition of words or phrases at the start of successive clauses.
'We shall fight on the beaches. We shall fight on the landing grounds. We shall fight in the fields, and in the streets, we shall fight in the hills. We shall never surrender.'

SHAKESPEARE'S PLAYS

Considerable debate still remains as to the chronology of Shakespeare's plays. The following is one account of the possible dates of composition:

The Comedy of Errors	1590[C]	Much Ado About Nothing	1599[C]
Titus Andronicus	1590[T]	Julius Caesar	1599[T]
The Taming of the Shrew	1591[C]	Twelfth Night	1600[C]
Henry VI Part 2	1591[H]	Hamlet	1601[T]
Henry VI Part 3	1591[H]	Troilus and Cressida	1602[C]
Henry VI Part 1	1592[H]	All's Well That Ends Well	1603[C]
Richard III	1592[H]	Measure for Measure	1604[C]
Love's Labour's Lost	1593[C]	Othello	1604[T]
Two Gentlemen of Verona	1593[C]	King Lear	1605[T]
A Midsummer Night's Dream	1594[C]	Macbeth	1605[T]
Romeo and Juliet	1595[T]	Antony and Cleopatra	1606[T]
Richard II	1595[H]	Timon of Athens	1606[T]
King John	1596[H]	Pericles, Prince of Tyre	1607[R]
The Merchant of Venice	1596[C]	Coriolanus	1608[T]
Henry IV Part 1	1597[H]	Cymbeline	1609[R]
The Merry Wives of Windsor	1597[C]	A Winter's Tale	1610[R]
Henry IV Part 2	1598[H]	The Tempest	1611[R]
As You Like It	1598[C]	Henry VIII	1613[H]
Henry V	1599[H]	(Two Noble Kinsmen)	1613[C]

Key: [C]omedy · [T]ragedy · [H]istory · [R]omance

FAMOUS CAT & DOG OWNERS

'I have had cats whom I liked better than this…but he is a very fine cat'[†]	*'Histories are more full of the examples of the fidelity of dogs than of friends'*[‡]
SAMUEL JOHNSON[†] . . . . Hodge	ALEXANDER POPE[‡] . . . . Bounce
EDWARD LEAR . . . . Foss	LORD BYRON . . . . Boatswain
THE KENNEDYS . . . . Tom Kitten	ISAAC NEWTON . . . . Diamond
CHARLES DE GAULLE . . . . Gris Gris	BILL CLINTON . . . . Buddy
CARDINAL RICHELIEU . . . Perruque	CHRISTOPHER MARLOWE Bungey
DOWNING STREET . . . . Humphrey	HOGARTH . . . . Trump
JOHN LENNON . . . . Elvis	THE QUEEN . . . . Susan[§]
CHURCHILL . . . . Margate, Jock	JULES VERNE . . . . Satellite
ALICE . . . . Dinah	SPUTNIK II . . . . Laika
MARK TWAIN . . . . Beelzebub	MARTIN CRANE . . . . Eddie
T.S. ELIOT . . . . . George Pushdragon	PETER MANDELSON . . . . Bobby
NICHOLAS I . . . . Vashka	[§] *The Queen's 1st corgi; an 18th-birthday gift*

ZODIAC DATES

F	Aries . . . . March 21 – April 20 . . . . Ram	♂
E	Taurus . . . . April 21 – May 21 . . . . Bull	♀
A	Gemini . . . . May 22 – June 21 . . . . Twins	♂
W	Cancer . . . . June 22 – July 23 . . . . Crab	♀
F	Leo . . . . July 24 – August 23 . . . . Lion	♂
E	Virgo . . . . August 24 – September 23 . . . . Virgin	♀
A	Libra . . . . September 24 – October 23 . . . . Scales	♂
W	Scorpio . . . . October 24 – November 22 . . . . Scorpion	♀
F	Sagittarius . . . . . . November 23 – December 22 . . . . Archer	♂
E	Capricorn . . . . . . December 23 – January 20 . . . . Goat	♀
A	Aquarius . . . . January 21 – February 19 . . . . . Water Carrier	♂
W	Pisces . . . . February 20 – March 20 . . . . Fish	♀

[*Dates change from year to year.*] · [F]ire · [E]arth · [A]ir · [W]ater · ♂ masculine · ♀ feminine

BISHOP'S SIGNATURES

Bishops of the Church of England sign their first name, and that of their See. For some older dioceses, the archaic Latin abbreviation is employed:

Signature	*Diocese*		
CANTAUR . . . . Canterbury	ROFFEN . . . . Rochester
EBOR . . . . York	SARUM . . . . Salisbury
PETRIBURG . . . . Peterborough	WINTON . . . . Winchester
	DUNELM . . . . Durham

CLOUD TYPES

ALTOSTRATUS
[As] 2000–7000m
Sheets of grey-blue cloud covering the sky, often obscuring sun & moon.

ALTOCUMULUS
[Ac] 2000–7000m
Patches and sheets of rounded or rolled cloud — separate or merged.

CIRROSTRATUS
[Cs] 5000–13700m
Sheets of cloud covering much of sky, sometimes giving a 'halo' effect.

CIRROCUMULUS
[Cc] 5000–13700m
'Mackerel sky' – grains or ripples of white cloud in regular patterns.

CIRRUS
[Ci] 5000–13700m
High, detached, white filaments or fibres of delicate, wispy cloud.

CUMULONIMBUS
[Cb] 460–2000m
Heavy, dense cloud with huge tall towers and dark shadows at base.

CUMULUS
[Cu] 460–2000m
Heaped, cauliflower shape; brilliant white areas with dark bases.

STRATUS
[St] surface–460m
Uniform low grey cloud, outline of sun & moon visible if cloud is thin.

STRATOCUMULUS
[Sc] 460–2000m
Layers of white cloud with dark grey areas; often light rain or snow.

NIMBOSTRATUS
[Ns] 900–3000m
Associated with rain & snow, covers most of the sky; dark and heavy.

In his essay 'On the Modification of Clouds', Luke Howard (1772–1864) employed four Latin terms to categorise the clouds he saw around him; these terms still form the basis of modern cloud taxonomy: cumulus, heap · stratus, layer · cirrus, curl · nimbus, rain.

——————— POST-WAR BRITISH ELECTIONS ———————

Election Date	Majority	% Turnout	Women MPs	% Women MPs	% Spoilt Papers	Winning Party
05.07.1945	146	72.7	24	3.8		Labour
23.02.1950	5	84.0	21	3.4		Labour
25.10.1951	17	82.5	17	2.7		Conservative
26.05.1955	58	76.7	24	3.8		Conservative
08.10.1959	100	78.8	25	4.0		Conservative
15.10.1964	4	77.1	29	4.6	0.15	Labour
31.03.1966	96	75.8	26	4.1	0.18	Labour
18.06.1970	30	72.0	26	4.1	0.15	Conservative
28.02.1974	-33	78.8	23	3.6	0.13	Labour
10.10.1974	3	72.8	27	4.3	0.13	Labour
03.05.1979	43	76.0	19	3.0	0.38	Conservative
09.06.1983	144	72.7	23	3.5	0.17	Conservative
11.06.1987	102	75.3	41	6.3	0.11	Conservative
09.04.1992	21	77.7	60	9.2	0.12	Conservative
01.05.1997	179	71.5	120	18.2	0.30	Labour
07.06.2001	166	59.4	118	17.9		Labour

——————— PENCIL HARDNESS ———————

The process of determining pencil hardness dates back to the work of Nicolas-Jacques Conté, who (*c.*1795) developed techniques for controlling the ratio of clay to graphite in pencil manufacture. The Conté grading system was a numerical scale where 1 was the hardest and 4 the softest. Later, British manufacturers developed their own letter-based grading system with softer leads given a B (for 'black') preface, and harder leads prefaced H (for 'hard'). Over time, these two scales have been combined to create a scale used widely across Europe and occasionally in America:

hardest — 9H, 8H, 7H … 2H, H, F, HB, B, 2B … 7B, 8B, 9B — *softest*

Many US pencil manufacturers, however, use a numerical code which inverts Conté's gradings, making #1 the softest, and #4 the hardest. A rough chart of equivalence between the two systems can be shown thus:

softest — #1 = B, #2 = HB, #2½ = F, #3 = H, #4 = 2H — *hardest*

All of these grading systems are to some extent arbitrary, since no strict or formal definitions of pencil hardness have ever been universally adopted.

——CONVERSIONS ANCIENT & MODERN——

CAPACITY

Scotch pint ...... 105 cubic inches
Barrel of soap .... 256 lbs
Barrel of herrings .... 32 lbs
Tub of butter .... 84 lbs
Soldier's canteen .... 3 pints
Gallipoli oil Salma .... 14.232 gills
Bordeaux Barreque ..... 51.61 gills
Cadiz Fanega .... 1.55 bushels
Trieste Stajo .... 0.691 bushels
Scotch Boll .... 1 English sack

WEIGHT

24 grains .... 1 pennyweight
Drop .... 1 grain
Bale .... 90 lbs
12 sacks .... 1 last
Last .... 39 cwt
Truss of hay .... 60 lbs
Man's load .... 5 bushels
Market load .... 40 bushels
Napels Picollo .... 7420 grains
Bengal Maund .... 120 lbs
Bazar Maund .... 82 lbs
Mysore Cutcha Seer .... 9 oz
Seam of glass .... 120 lbs
Bassora Biscal .... 72 grains
Chaldron .... 28 cwt

BIBLICAL MEASURES

Cubitt .... 21.8"
Omer .... 0.45 peck
Ephan .... 10 omers
Schekel .... 14.1 grams

LENGTH

48 hair's-breadths .... 1"
3 barleycorns (lengthways) ...... 1"
Nail .... 2½"
Hand .... 4"
Palm .... 3"
Span .... 9"
Pole .... 5½ yards
Fathom .... 6'
Pace .... 4'4"
French Toise .... 6.395'
Guinean Jacktam .... 4 yards
Chinese Covid .... 14.62"
Indian Candi .... 2'1"
Levantine Pig .... 2'4"
Jaghire .... 10.46"
Greek Studium .... 600'
Olympic Foot .... 12¾"
Greek Acaena .... 10 foot-rod
Chain .... 4 poles
Ox gang .... 15 acres
Hide of land .... 100–120 acres

MODERN CONVERSION MULTIPLICATIONS

IMPERIAL	imperial to metric multiply by	metric to imperial multiply by	METRIC
inches	2.54	0.3937	centimetres
feet	0.3048	3.2808	metres
yards	0.9144	1.0936	metres
miles	1.6093	0.6214	kilometres
acres	0.4047	2.471	hectares
square miles	2.5899	0.386	square kilometres
UK pints	0.5682	1.7598	litres
UK gallons	4.546	0.2199	litres
pounds	0.4536	2.2046	kilograms
tons (long)	1.016	0.9842	tonnes

———— ART STYLES: GOTHIC TO CUBISM ————

GOTHIC (C12th–16th) Detailed & devotional: pointed stone arches, stained glass and ribbed vaulting. (C16th) INTERNATIONAL GOTHIC Late-medieval art style. [*Pisanello*]

RENAISSANCE (C14th–16th) The classical revival in learning & all manner of sculpture, art, and architecture. Oil painting and use of perspective were developed. [*Botticelli, da Vinci, Ghiberti*]

MANNERISM (mid–late C16th) An exaggeration of the Renaissance, which grew overly extravagant and stylised. [*Michelangelo, Bronzino*]

BAROQUE (C17th) Encouraged by the Roman Catholic Church, the Baroque style unified the various forms of art and architecture, creating realistic & dramatic work. [*Caravaggio, Bernini, Rubens*]

ROCOCO (mid–late C18th) A highly ornate and lightweight, decorative style, developed in part at the court of King Louis XV. [*Watteau, Fragonard, Tiepolo*]

NEO-CLASSICISM (1750–1850) A return to Greek classical formality in art & architecture in a response to (and rejection of) Baroque and Rococo.[*Piranesi, Adam, Soane*]

ROMANTICISM (1780–1850) The championing of human emotion, and the inspiration of the natural world in reaction to industry and the Enlightenment. [*Turner, Blake Delacroix, Constable*]

ARTS & CRAFTS (1850–1870) Anti-industrial revival of authentic decorative, and functional craft, for social reform. [*William Morris*]

IMPRESSIONISM (1860s–80s) The exploration of colour & technique to capture the transience of light. [*Monet, Sisley, Pissaro, Renoir*]

POINTILLISM (1880s) Painting style using small dots of primary colour which merge to form an image. [*Seurat, Signac, Cross*]

POST-IMPRESSIONISM (1880–1910) A move away from Impressionistic representation, towards a more abstract and emotional approach. [*Cézanne, Gauguin, van Gogh*]

ART NOUVEAU (1890–1915) Detailed decorative style, using both fluid curved lines, and strict geometry. [*Beardsley, Klimt, Tiffany*]

FAUVISM (1900–1908) The French 'movement' championing daring, bold, colourful & exuberant work. [*Matisse, Rouault, Dufy*]

EXPRESSIONISM (1900–40s) A style emphasising the emotions and responses of the artist, rather than the realistic depiction of a subject. [*Kandinsky, Grosz, Modigliani*]

CUBISM (1900s–20s) Developed by *Picasso* and *Braque*, and influenced by Cézanne and tribal art, Cubism sought ways to see the essence of the subject by showing all of its fragmented facets simultaneously.

SOME NOTABLE BELGIANS

Jean Aerts	*cyclist*	Cornelius Jansen	*theologian*
Jules Bordet	*scientist*	Roland de Lassus	*composer*
Hieronymus Bosch	*painter*	René Magritte	*painter*
Thiery Boutsen	*racing driver*	Eddy Merckx	*cyclist*
Jacques Brel	*singer*	Christophe Plantin	*typographer*
Pieter Breughel	*painter*	Plastique Bertrand	*musician*
Ernest Claes	*writer*	Georges Rémi	*creator of Tin Tin*
Pierre Culliford	*'Smurfs' creator*	Peter Paul Rubens	*painter*
Paul Delvaux	*painter*	Adolphe Sax	*saxophone inventor*
Lamoral Egmont	*statesman*	Georges Simenon	*writer*
Audrey Hepburn	*actress*	Jean-Claude Van Damme	*actor*

BOOKS OF THE 1830 BOOK OF MORMON

First Nephi	Omni	Third Nephi
Second Nephi	Words of Mormon	Fourth Nephi
Jacob	Mosiah	Mormon
Enos	Alma	Ether
Jarom	Helaman	Moroni

CONTRADICTORY PROVERBS

Beware of Greeks bearing gifts	*Don't look a gift horse in the mouth*
Many hands make light work	*Too many cooks spoil the broth*
No fool like an old fool	*With age comes wisdom*
Tomorrow's another day	*Tomorrow never comes*
Two heads are better than one	*Two of a trade never agree*
Great minds think alike	*Idiots seldom differ*
Fools rush in where angels fear to tread	*He who hesitates is lost*
Absence makes the heart grow fonder	*Out of sight, out of mind*
The tailor maketh the man	*Never judge a book by its cover*
You're never too old to learn	*You can't teach an old dog new tricks*
Familiarity breeds contempt	*Better the devil you know*

DOCTORS WHO

William Hartnell	1963–66	Peter Davison	1980–84
Patrick Troughton	1966–69	Colin Baker	1984–86
Jon Pertwee	1969–73	Sylvester McCoy	1986–96
Tom Baker	1974–80	Paul McGann	1996

———————————— U AND NON-U ————————————

In 1954, Prof. Alan Ross published his essay 'Linguistic class-indicators in present-day English' in the renowned Finnish philological journal, *Neuphilologische Mitteilungen*. Here, Ross attempted to codify the spoken and written linguistic rules which demarcated upper-class language. His premise was that very subtle norms of phrasing, pronunciation, or vocabulary would instantly distinguish an upper-class ('U') speaker from the working or aspirational middle-class ('non-U') speaker – as below:

NON-U	U		
to take a bath ...... to have a bath		perfume....................... scent
cycle .... bicycle		note-paper .... writing-paper
dinner....................... lunch		pardon? .... what?
supper....................... dinner		preserve .... jam
dress suit .... dinner jacket		business/calling card.......... card
greens.................... vegetables		radio .... wireless
horse-riding................. riding		serviette.............. table-napkin
jack (at cards) .... knave		toilet....................... lavatory
home....................... house		wealthy .... rich
mirror .... looking-glass		sweet .... pudding
		wire .... telegram

———————————— 1/299,792,458 ————————————

Since 1983, the *metre* has been defined internationally as the length of the path travelled by light in a vacuum during 1/299,792,458th of a second. Importantly, a *second* is in turn defined as the duration of 9,192,631,770 periods of the radiation corresponding to the transition between the two hyperfine levels of the ground state of the caesium-133 atom.

———————————— MEASURING BRA SIZES ————————————

First, whilst wearing a bra, measure around the rib cage, directly under your bust. Add 5"to odd numbers, and 4" to even numbers. This is your band or bra size, e.g. 31"+5"=36" or 34"+4"=38". Then, measure the fullest part of the bust. The difference between the full bust measurement and the band or bra size gives the cupsize as the following table indicates:

difference .... *cup size*	3" > bra size.................... D
1"< bra size .... AA	4" > bra size.................... DD
= bra size .... A	5" > bra size .... E
1" > bra size .... B	6" > bra size .... F
2" > bra size.................... C	7" > bra size.................... G

———— SCHEMATIC OF DANTE'S INFERNO ————

Some Inhabitants	*Region of Hell*	*Punishment*
Leopard, lion, she-wolf	FOREST	
Pope Celestine V	VESTIBULE	Pursued by insects
[Charon, the ferryman]	*~ River Acheron ~*	*'Upper Hell'*
Homer, Socrates, Plato	1 — LIMBO — 1	Desire without hope
[Minòs] Dido, Cleopatra	2 — THE LUSTFUL — 2	Battered by violent winds
[Cerberus] Ciacco	3 — THE GLUTTONOUS — 3	Besieged by foul weather
[Plutus]	4 — THE AVARICIOUS — 4	Perpetual violence
	THE ANGRY & SULLEN	Submerged in Styx
	5 — — 5	
[Phlegyas, the boatman]	*~ River Styx ~*	*'Lower Hell', City of Dis*
	THE HERETICS	
Frederick II	6 — — 6	Burned in tombs
[Minotaur]	7 — THE VIOLENT — 7	
[Centaurs]	*~ River Phlegethon ~*	
Alexander, Attila	*Violent against Others*	Drowned in hot blood
della Vigna, Lano Da Siena	*Suicides and Squanderers*	Enclosed in trees
Capaneus	*Violent against God or Nature*	Burned on hot sands
Brunetto Latini	*Unnatural Lust*	Forced perpetually to run
[Geryon]	8 — SIMPLE FRAUD — 8	*'Maleboge'*
Venedico Caccianemico	*Panderers & Seducers*	Whipped to walk endlessly
Alessio Interminei, Thais	*Flatterers*	Sunk in excrement
Pope Nicholas III	*Simoniacs*	Inverted and burned
Tiresias, Guido Bonatti	*Astrologers and Magicians*	Heads twisted round
[Malacoda &c.] Ciampolo	*Barrators*	Burned with pitch
Caiaphas, Annas	*Hypocrites*	Clad in weights
Vanni Fucci, Cacus	*Thieves*	Attacked by serpents
Ulysses, Diomed	*Fraudulent Counsellors*	Burned with flames
Bertram De Born	*Sowers of Discord*	Endlessly mutilated
Gianni Schicchi, Sinon	*Alchemists, Falsifiers*	Pain, filth, disease, attack
Nimrod, Antaeus, Ephialtes	THE GIANTS	Bound in chains
	~ Frozen Lake of River Cocytus ~	*'Cocytus'*
	9 — TREACHEROUS FRAUD — 9	
Napoleone Degli Alberti	*Traitors to Kin*	Up to shoulders in ice
Archbishop Ruggieri	*Traitors to Country*	Up to neck in ice
Branca D'Oria	*Traitors to Guests*	Immersed in ice
Judas, Brutus, Cassius	*Traitors to Benefactors & God*	Held in Lucifer's mouth

† LUCIFER †

———— BEATLES' UK NUMBER ONE SINGLES ————

Year	Title	Weeks	Length	First release on album
63	From Me To You	7	1:54	*Oldies (But Goldies)*
63	She Loves You	6 †	2:18	*Oldies (But Goldies)*
63	I Want To Hold Your Hand	5 † *	2:22	*Oldies (But Goldies)*
64	Can't Buy Me Love	3 †	2:10	*A Hard Day's Night*
64	A Hard Day's Night	3 †	2:29	*A Hard Day's Night*
64	I Feel Fine	5 † *	2:17	*Oldies (But Goldies)*
65	Ticket To Ride	3 †	3:09	*Help!*
65	Help!	3 †	2:16	*Help!*
65	Day Tripper *& We Can Work It Out*	5 † *	2:49	*Oldies (But Goldies)*
66	Paperback Writer	2 †	2:15	*Oldies (But Goldies)*
66	Yellow Submarine *& Eleanor Rigby*	4	2:36	*Revolver*
67	All You Need Is Love	3 †	3:47	*Magical Mystery Tour*
67	Hello Goodbye	7 † *	3:27	*Magical Mystery Tour*
68	Lady Madonna	2	2:14	*The 'Blue Album'*
68	Hey Jude!	2 †	7:07	*The 'Blue Album'*
69	Get Back	6 †	3:06	*Let It Be*
69	Ballad Of John And Yoko	3	2:58	*The 'Blue Album'*

Key: † also Number One in the USA · * Christmas Number One
Some charts give 'Please Please Me' as Number One in 1963.

———— WEATHER PROVERBS ————

Red sky at night, shepherds' delight, red sky in the morning, shepherds' warning.

Rain before seven, fine by eleven.

Evening red and morning grey, two sure signs of a perfect day.

March winds and April showers bring forth May flowers.

The sudden storm lasts not three hours.

Clear moon, frost soon.

The higher the clouds, the better the weather.

Halo around the sun or moon, rain or snow is coming soon.

Cold is the night when the stars shine bright.

One swallow does not a summer make.

The farther the sight, the nearer the rain.

Dew on the grass, rain shan't pass.

APOTHECARIES' CONVERSIONS

WEIGHTS	MEASURES
20 grains .... 1 scruple	20 minims............ 1 fl. scruple
3 scruples .... 1 drachm	3 fl. scruples .... 1 fl. drachm
8 drachms .... 1 ounce	8 fl. drachms........... 1 fl. ounce
12 ounces............... 1 pound	20 fl. ounces............... 1 pint

SUPPLIERS TO THE QUEEN

CHOCOLATE MANUFACTURERS....................	*Charbonnel et Walker*
GREENGROCER AND FLORIST................	*Aboyne & Ballater Flowers*
BESOM BROOMS & PEA STICKS................................	*A. Nash*
POTTED SHRIMPS	*James Baxter & Son*
FRUIT JUICES & SOFT DRINKS	*Britvic Soft Drinks*
BISCUIT MANUFACTURERS	*William Crawford & Sons*
CANDLEMAKERS................................	*Price's Patent Candle Co.*
MOTOR LUBRICANTS..	*Castrol*
BUTCHERS...	*Cobb of Knightsbridge*
WINE MERCHANTS	*Corney & Barrow*
SCOTCH WHISKY DISTILLERS.................	*William Sanderson & Son*
PORK SAUSAGES................................	*Fairfax Meadow Farm*
CHEESEMAKERS....................................	*Howgate Dairy Foods*
GROCERS & PROVISIONS	*Fortnum & Mason*
STATIONERS	*Frank Smythson*
COACH PAINTS	*Akzo Nobel C.T. Coatings*
PICTURE FRAMERS	*Petersfield Book Shop*
PIANOFORTE MANUFACTURERS.................	*John Broadwood & Sons*
BAGPIPE MAKERS	*R.G. Hardie & Co*
RESTORER OF FINE-ART OBJECTS	*Plowden & Smith*
FINE-ART DEALERS............................	*Hazlitt Gooden & Fox*
ANGOSTURA BITTERS	*Angostura Ltd*
ROSES..	*James Cocker & Sons*
PHILATELISTS..	*Stanley Gibbons*
GUNSMITHS..	*Gallyon & Sons*
BOOKSELLERS..	*Alden & Blackwell*
BRASS FINISHERS & SPRING MAKERS	*Cope & Timmins*
CHRISTMAS CRACKERS................................	*Tom Smith Group*

SEVEN SEAS

Antarctic · Arctic · North Atlantic · South Atlantic
Indian Ocean · North Pacific · South Pacific

—————— PHILATELIC GLOSSARY ——————

Below are a few of the many terms used by stamp dealers and collectors.

ALBINO a stamp rendered colourless by a printing error.

PHOSPHOR marks or bands of a fluorescent substance to be read by automatic sorting machines.

BISECT a stamp legitimately cut in half to pay postage at half the rate.

CACHET a handstamp used to commemorate a special edition.

SE-TENANT two or more stamps issued joined together but with different values or designs, often used to form composite designs.

TÊTE-BÊCHE a pair of adjoined stamps, one upside-down.

DRY PRINT a stamp with a weak or pale image due to insufficient ink.

ERROR stamps erroneously issued with incorrect designs.

PLATE NUMBER an identifying mark in the margin of a sheet.

FISCAL STAMPS a stamp issued for the collection of tax.

SURCHARGE an overprint which changes the face value of a stamp.

—————— CREASY'S DECISIVE BATTLES ——————

In his 1851 book, *The Fifteen Decisive Battles of the World*, Professor Sir Edward Shepherd Creasy (1812–78) gave his analysis of the moments of conflict which he claimed for ever changed the course of world history.

Date	Battle	Decisive Action
BC 490	Marathon	*Greeks under Militades defeated the Persians*
413	Syracuse	*Peloponnesian War limiting Greek expansion*
331	Arbela	*Alexander overthrew Darius*
207	Metarus	*Romans defeated Hannibal*
AD 9	Arminius	*Gauls overthrew the Romans*
451	Châlons	*Attila's defeat by Actius*
732	Tours	*Charles Martel overthrew the Saracens*
1066	Hastings	*Norman Conquest of England*
1429	Orléans	*Joan of Arc secured French independence*
1588	Spanish Armada	*England's defeat of the Spanish*
1704	Blenheim	*Marlborough's defeat of Tallard*
1709	Pultowa	*Russia's defeat of Sweden*
1777	Saratoga	*Gates defeated Burgoyne*
1792	Valmy	*Revolutionists' defeat of allies under Brunswick*
1815	Waterloo	*Wellington's defeat of Napoleon*

KNIGHTS OF THE ROUND TABLE

According to Dryden, there were 12 knights; Sir Walter Scott named 16. The 10 given below seem to be accepted by most writers on the subject:

Lancelot · Tristram · Lamorack · Tor · Galahad
Gawain · Palomides · Kay · Mark · Mordred

RUGBY UNION PLAYING POSITIONS

Loosehead Prop · Hooker · Tighthead Prop
Second Row · Second Row
Blindside Flanker · Number 8 · Openside Flanker

Scrum Half

Fly Half

Inside Centre

Left Wing   Outside Centre

Right Wing

Full Back

MULTIPLE NOBEL PRIZE WINNERS

The Nobel Prize is the bequest of Alfred Nobel (1833–96), the inventor of dynamite. Since 1901, prizes have been awarded annually for significant achievements in chemistry, physics, medicine, literature, and peace. Very few people, or organisations, have been awarded more than one prize:

MARIE CURIE
1903 *Physics* · 1911 *Chemistry*

THE RED CROSS
1917 *Peace* · 1944 *Peace*
1963 *Peace*

LINUS PAULING
1954 *Chemistry* · 1962 *Peace*

FREDERICK SANGER
1958 *Chemistry* · 1980 *Chemistry*

UN HIGH COMMISSION
FOR REFUGEES
1954 *Peace* · 1981 *Peace*

JOHN BARDEEN
1956 *Physics* · 1972 *Physics*

TEST CRICKET NATIONS

Australia · Bangladesh · England · India · New Zealand · Pakistan
South Africa · Sri Lanka · West Indies · Zimbabwe

CHINESE ZODIAC YEARS

RAT · 1912 · 1924 · 1936 · 1948 · 1960 · 1972 · 1984 · 1996 · 2008

OX · 1913 · 1925 · 1937 · 1949 · 1961 · 1973 · 1985 · 1997 · 2009

TIGER · 1914 · 1926 · 1938 · 1950 · 1962 · 1974 · 1986 · 1998 · 2010

RABBIT · 1915 · 1927 · 1939 · 1951 · 1963 · 1975 · 1987 · 1999 · 2011

DRAGON · 1916 · 1928 · 1940 · 1952 · 1964 · 1976 · 1988 · 2000 · 2012

SNAKE · 1917 · 1929 · 1941 · 1953 · 1965 · 1977 · 1989 · 2001 · 2013

HORSE · 1918 · 1930 · 1942 · 1954 · 1966 · 1978 · 1990 · 2002 · 2014

RAM · 1919 · 1931 · 1943 · 1955 · 1967 · 1979 · 1991 · 2003 · 2015

MONKEY · 1920 · 1932 · 1944 · 1956 · 1968 · 1980 · 1992 · 2004 · 2016

ROOSTER · 1921 · 1933 · 1945 · 1957 · 1969 · 1981 · 1993 · 2005 · 2017

DOG · 1922 · 1934 · 1946 · 1958 · 1970 · 1982 · 1994 · 2006 · 2018

BOAR/PIG · 1923 · 1935 · 1947 · 1959 · 1971 · 1983 · 1995 · 2007 · 2019

SPECIFICATIONS OF THE ARK

Made from	gopherwood	Decks	3
Length	300 cubits	Number of humans	8
Breadth	50 cubits	Rain duration	40 days & nights
Height	30 cubits	Flood prevailed for	150 days
Windows	1	Noah lived to	950 years

CHESS TERMS

BAD BISHOP A bishop unable to move freely because of friendly pawns, themselves unable to move.

BASE OF PAWN CHAIN the last and weakest pawn in a diagonal chain.

BURIED PIECE one hemmed in by friendly pieces.

CASTLE moving the king two squares either right or left, and placing the rook on the square beside the king closest to the centre.

CENTRE the four centre squares.

DEVELOPMENT bringing pieces into play.

DIAGONAL lines moved by bishops and queens from North East to South West, or from North West to South East.

DISCOVERED CHECK check given by one piece as the result of the moving away of another piece that was masking it.

DOUBLED PAWNS two pawns of the same colour on the same file.

EN PASSANT where a pawn on the 5th rank captures an opponent's pawn on an adjacent file, which has just moved 2 squares forward on its first move.

EN PRISE an unprotected piece vulnerable to capture.

FILE a vertical row of squares.

J'ADOUBE or I ADJUST said to warn that a piece is merely being adjusted and not actually played.

PERPETUAL CHECK an endless attack on a king which will not lead to checkmate. Often this position results in a draw.

PIN a piece which masks another from attack.

PROMOTION a pawn which reaches the final rank can be 'promoted' to a queen, rook, bishop, or knight (usually a queen – hence the alternate term often employed: QUEENING).

RANK a horizontal row of squares.

SACRIFICE (or SAC) the deliberate loss of a piece for tactical gain.

SANS VOIR playing blindfolded.

SKEWER when a piece is forced to move exposing another piece to capture.

STALEMATE a drawn game where no legal move is playable.

WAITING MOVE a benign move designed to change the turn.

ZUGZWANG a position whereby any move is disadvantageous.

ZWISCHENZUG an unexpected move played within a sequence.

—————— SOME PHILOSOPHICAL QUOTATIONS ——————

FRIEDRICH NIETZSCHE · God is dead: but considering the state the species of Man is in, there will perhaps be caves, for ages yet, in which his shadow will be shown.

SIGMUND FREUD · Anatomy is destiny.

MICHAEL OAKESHOTT · Anyone who has had a glimpse of the range and subtlety of the thought of Plato or of Hegel will long ago have despaired of becoming a philosopher.

THOMAS HOBBES · [*on the state of nature*] No arts; no letters; no society; and which is worst of all, continual fear and danger of violent death; and the life of man, solitary, poor, nasty, brutish and short.

RENÉ DESCARTES · *Cogito ergo sum* (I think therefore I am).

CICERO · The good of the people is the chief law.

ADAM SMITH · Science is the great antidote to the poison of enthusiasm and superstition.

JEREMY BENTHAM · The greatest happiness of the greatest number is the foundation of morals and legislation.

ARISTOTLE · Poetry is more philosophical and more serious than history, for its statements are in the nature of universals, whereas those of history are singulars.

IMMANUEL KANT · Out of the crooked tree of humanity no straight thing can ever be made.

BENEDICT SPINOZA · All noble things are as difficult as they are rare.

BERTRAND RUSSELL · If one man offers you democracy and another offers you a bag of grain, at what stage of starvation will you prefer the grain to the vote?

BLAISE PASCAL · I lay it down as a fact that if all men knew what others say of them, there would not be four friends in the world.

DIONYSIUS OF HALICARNASSUS History is philosophy derived from examples.

ÉMILE DURKHEIM · There is no society known where a more or less developed criminality is not found under different forms.

WILLIAM OF OCCAM · No more things should be presumed to exist than are absolutely necessary.

JEAN-PAUL SARTRE · Everything is gratuitous, this garden, this city and myself. When you suddenly realise it, it makes you feel sick and everything begins to drift ... that's nausea.

HENRY DAVID THOREAU · Some circumstantial evidence is very strong, as when you find a trout in the milk.

——— PHILOSOPHICAL QUOTATIONS cont. ———

ERICH FROMM · There is perhaps no phenomenon which contains so much destructive feeling as 'moral indignation', which permits envy or hate to be acted out under the guise of virtue.

FRIEDRICH ENGELS · The State is not 'abolished', it withers away.

GEORGE BERKELEY · Truth is the cry of all, but the game of few.

THEODORE ADORNO · The total effect of the culture industry is one of anti-enlightenment ... the progressive technical domination of nature, becomes mass deception and is turned into a means for fettering consciousness.

GEORG HEGEL · When philosophy paints its grey on grey, then has a shape of life grown old. By philosophy's grey on grey it cannot be rejuvenated but only understood. The owl of Minerva spreads its wings only with the falling of the dusk.

LUDWIG WITTGENSTEIN · The face is the soul of the body.

ISAIAH BERLIN · The fundamental sense of freedom is freedom from chains, from imprisonment, from enslavement by others. The rest is extension of this sense, or else metaphor.

GEORGE BERNARD SHAW · There is only one religion, though there are a hundred versions of it.

SOCRATES · The unexamined life is not worth living.

THOMAS AQUINAS · Man has free choice, or otherwise counsels, exhortations, commands, prohibitions, rewards and punishments would be in vain.

GOTTFRIED LEIBNITZ · There are two kinds of truths: those of reasoning and those of fact. The truths of reasoning are necessary and their opposite is impossible; the truths of fact are contingent and their opposites are possible.

KARL POPPER · In so far as a scientific statement speaks about reality, it must be falsifiable: and in so far as it is not falsifiable, it does not speak about reality.

FRANCIS BACON · If a man will begin with certainties, he shall end in doubts; but if he will be content to begin with doubts, he shall end in certainties.

J.S. MILL · War is an ugly thing, but not the ugliest of things: the decayed and degraded state of moral and patriotic feeling which thinks nothing worth a war, is worse.

MARCUS AURELIUS · Every instant of time is a pinprick of eternity. All things are petty, easily changed, vanishing away.

LEO TOLSTOY· Friedrich Nietzsche was stupid and abnormal.

POTENTIAL OF HYDROGEN

pH *(Potential of Hydrogen)* is a measure of acidity and alkalinity. The pH is defined as the negative logarithm of the hydrogen-ion concentration: or $pH=\log_{10}1/[H^+]$. The pH of pure water is 7 or neutral ($\log_{10}1/[10^{-7}]$); acids have a pH<7; and alkalies have a pH>7. The scale is logarithmic, so pH1 is 10x more acidic than pH2. Below are some approximate values:

0.1	hydrochloric acid	6.4	saliva
0.3	sulphuric acid	6.8	milk
1.0	stomach acid	7.0	distilled water
2.3	lemon juice	7.2	blood
2.8	vinegar	8.0	seawater
5.0	black coffee	9.0	baking soda
5.2	acid rain	10.5	milk of magnesia
5.5	white bread	11.0	domestic bleach
5.7	rainwater	14.0	caustic soda

COOKING TEMPERATURES

Description	°C	°F	Gas Mark	Aga[†] Setting
very slow	110	225	¼	very cool
	120	250	½	
	140	275	1	
slow	150	300	2	cool
	160–70	325	3	warm
moderate	180	350	4	
	190	375	5	medium
moderate hot	200	400	6	medium high
	220	425	7	
hot	230	450	8	high
very hot	240–60	475	9	very high

† 'Aga' is an acronym derived from the maker: *Svenska [A]ktienbolaget [G]as[a]kumulator Co.*

THE HIERARCHY OF FALCONRY

In her idiosyncratic 1486 *Boke of St Albans*, Dame Julia Berners presents a hierarchy of hawks and the social ranks with which they are appropriate:

Gerfalcon	King	Merlin	Lady
Peregrine Falcon	Earl	Tercel	Poorman
Bastard Hawk	Baron	Sparrowhawk	Priest
Lanner & Lanneret	Squire	Kestrel	Servant or Knave

COMPASS POINTS

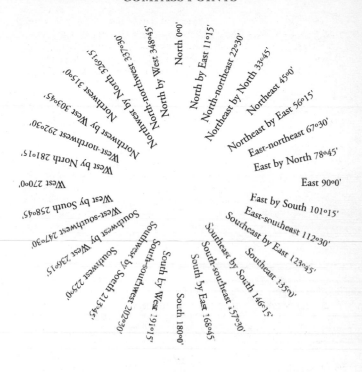

North 0°0'
North by East 11°15'
North-northeast 22°30'
Northeast by North 33°45'
Northeast 45°00'
Northeast by East 56°15'
East-northeast 67°30'
East by North 78°45'
East 90°0'
East by South 101°15'
East-southeast 112°30'
Southeast by East 123°45'
Southeast 135°0'
Southeast by South 146°15'
South-southeast 157°30'
South by East 168°45'
South 180°0'
South by West 191°15'
South-southwest 202°30'
Southwest by South 213°45'
Southwest 225°0'
Southwest by West 236°15'
West-southwest 247°30'
West by South 258°45'
West 270°0'
West by North 281°15'
West-northwest 292°30'
Northwest by West 303°45'
Northwest 315°0'
Northwest by North 326°15'
North-northwest 337°30'
North by West 348°45'

FREUD & THE MIND

ID (derived from the Latin word for 'It') is the elemental, unconscious and uncivilised mind. It is the centre of basic, primitive instincts and urges, and is geared towards selfishness and survival. The Id is best personified by the urges and behaviour of the new-born baby.

EGO (derived from the Latin for 'I') is the conscious and preconscious mind which civilises the Id, and recognises the existence of a wider world. The Ego represses inappropriate urges of the Id, and conflict between the Ego and the Id is the cause of neuroses.

SUPEREGO is the highest state of mind to which we have evolved. It is our conscience, regulating our thoughts and actions, checking the demands of the Id and the Ego. The Superego reacts and responds to the sophisticated rules and norms of society.

SOME LEFT-HANDERS

Lewis Carroll	Tiberius	Prince Charles	Paul Klee
Gary Sobers	George VI	Paul McCartney	Bob Dylan
Albert Einstein	Nietzsche	M.C. Escher	Bill Clinton
Bill Gates	Fidel Castro	Queen Victoria	H.G. Wells
Cole Porter	Pelé	Phil Collins	Elizabeth II

SNEEZING

If you sneeze on Monday, you sneeze for danger;
Sneeze on Tuesday, kiss a stranger;
Sneeze on Wednesday, sneeze for a letter;
Sneeze on Thursday, something better;
Sneeze on Friday, sneeze for sorrow;
Sneeze on Saturday, see your sweetheart tomorrow.

MILITARY HIERARCHY

BRITISH ARMY	ROYAL NAVY	ROYAL AIR FORCE
Officers	*Officers*	*Officers*
{Field Marshal}	Admiral of the Fleet	Marshall of the RAF
General	Admiral	Air Chief Marshal
Lieutenant-General	Vice-Admiral	Air Marshal
Major-General	Rear-Admiral	Air Vice-Marshal
Brigadier	Commodore	Air Commodore
Colonel	Captain	Group Captain
Lieutenant-Colonel	Commander	Wing Commander
Major	Lt.-Commander	Squadron Leader
Captain	Lieutenant	Flight Lieutenant
Lieutenant	Sub-Lieutenant	Flying Officer
Second Lieutenant	Midshipman	Pilot Officer
		Acting Pilot Officer
Other Ranks	*Other Ranks*	*Other Ranks*
Warrant Officer (cls 1)	Warrant Officer	Warrant Officer
Warrant Officer (cls 2)	Chief Petty Officer	Flight Sergeant/
Staff Sergeant	Petty Officer	Chief Technician
Sergeant	Leading Rating	Sergeant
Corporal	Able Rating	Corporal
Lance-Corporal	Ordinary Rating	Leading Aircraftman
Private		Aircraftman

CLOTHING CARE SYMBOLS

WASHING							
Maximum Temperature	Hand Wash	Bars under the washing symbol can have different meanings. Always check.	Cotton / Normal	Synthetics / Permapress	Wool / Gentle	Do not Wash	

BLEACHING					OTHER		
Chlorine bleach	Chlorine bleach	Non-chlorine bleach	Do not Bleach		No Heat or Air	Do not wring	

IRONING							
Iron on low	Iron on medium	Iron on high	Maximum temperature	Steam	No steam	Do not Iron	

DRYING							
Tumble dry low	Tumble dry medium	Tumble dry high	Drip-dry	Dry flat	Line-dry	Do not tumble dry	

DRY CLEANING						
Dry clean	Any solvent	Not trichloro-ethylene	Petroleum solvent	Additional markings give specialist information to professional dry-cleaners.	Do not dry clean	

Symbols and their meaning can vary around the world. Seek advice before cleaning.

COUNTRIES THAT DRIVE ON THE LEFT

Anguilla · Antigua · Australia · Bahamas · Bangladesh · Barbados
Bermuda · Bhutan · Botswana · British Virgin Islands · Brunei
Cayman Islands · Channel Islands · Ciskei · Cook Islands · Cyprus
Dominica · Falkland Islands · Fiji Islands · Grenada · Guyana
Hong Kong · India · Indonesia · Republic of Ireland · Jamaica · Japan
Kenya · Kiribati · Lesotho · Macau · Malawi · Malaysia · Malta
Mauritius · Montserrat · Mozambique · Namibia · Nepal · New Zealand
Niue · Norfolk Islands · Pakistan · Papua New Guinea · Seychelles
Sikkim · Singapore · Solomon Islds · Somalia · South Africa · Sri Lanka
St Helena · St Kitts & Nevis · St Lucia · St Vincent · Surinam
Swaziland · Tanzania · Thailand · Tonga · Trinidad & Tobago · Tuvalu
Uganda · UK[†] · US Virgin Islands · Venda · Zambia · Zimbabwe

[†] *Except in Savoy Street, off Strand in London, where traffic must drive on the right.*

THE PLANETS

Name	Diameter	No. of Moons	Surface Gravity	Rings?	Kms from Sun
MERCURY	4,878 km	0	370 cm/s²	no	57,909,175
VENUS	12,104	0	887	no	108,208,930
EARTH	12,756	1	980	no	149,597,890
MARS	6,794	2	371	no	227,936,640
JUPITER	142,800	39	2,312	yes	778,412,020
SATURN	120,536	30	896	yes	1,426,725,400
URANUS	51,118	20	869	yes	2,870,972,200
NEPTUNE	49,492	8	1,100	yes	4,498,252,900
PLUTO	2,300	1	81	no	5,906,376,200

SOLOMON GRUNDY

Solomon Grundy, Born on Monday,
Christened on Tuesday, Married on Wednesday,
Took ill on Thursday, Worse on Friday,
Died on Saturday, Buried on Sunday:
This is the end of Solomon Grundy.

CONTRADICTANYMS

Contradictanyms are words which have opposing meanings depending on the context in which they are used. For example, the word DUST can mean to add fine particles (as in *dust the cake with icing sugar*) as well as to remove fine particles (as in *dust the furniture*). Examples include:

You must BOLT the door .... or he will BOLT for the door
FLOG a horse........................... in order to FLOG the horse-meat
GARNISH that dish .... or I will GARNISH your earnings
Secure it with a BUCKLE .... or it will BUCKLE under the weight
Please SCREEN us from............... the film they are about to SCREEN
Though CRITICAL in his comments .... he was CRITICAL to our success
You can see the stars are OUT.................... once the lights are OUT
It is everyday CUSTOM .... to have suits CUSTOM-made
It was an OVERSIGHT .... to give him OVERSIGHT of the project
I will FIX the gate .... in order to FIX the race
Bind him FAST to prevent................................. a FAST getaway
He was only a QUALIFIED success....... although he is fully QUALIFIED

——— BRITISH PRIME MINISTERS ———

1997 .... Tony Blair [L]	1858 ...... Viscount Palmerston [Li]
1990 .... John Major [C]	1858 .... Edward Stanley [C]
1979 .... Margaret Thatcher [C]	1855 ...... Viscount Palmerston [Li]
1976 .... James Callaghan [L]	1852 ...... G. Hamilton-Gordon [C]
1974 .... Harold Wilson [L]	1852 .... Edward Stanley [C]
1970 .... Edward Heath [C]	1846 .... John Russell [W]
1964 .... Harold Wilson [L]	1841 .... Sir Robert Peel [T]
1963 .... Alec Douglas-Home [C]	1835 .... William Lamb [W]
1957 .... Harold Macmillan [C]	1834 .... Robert Peel [T]
1955 .... Sir Anthony Eden [C]	1834 .... Arthur Wellesley [T]
1951 .... Winston Churchill [C]	1834 .... William Lamb [W]
1945 .... Clement Attlee [L]	1830 .... Charles Grey [W]
1940 .... Winston Churchill [N/C]	1828 .... Arthur Wellesley [T]
1937 ...... Neville Chamberlain [N/C]	1827 .... Frederick Robinson [T]
1935 .... Stanley Baldwin [N/C]	1827 .... George Canning [T]
1931 .... Ramsay MacDonald [N]	1812 .... Robert Jenkinson [T]
1929 .... Ramsay MacDonald [L]	1809 .... Spencer Perceval [T]
1924 .... Stanley Baldwin [C]	1807 .... William Bentinck [T]
1924 .... Ramsay MacDonald [L]	1806 .... William Grenville [W]
1923 .... Stanley Baldwin [C]	1804 ... William Pitt [The Younger] [T]
1922 .... Andrew Bonar Law [C]	1801 .... Henry Addington [T]
1916 .... David Lloyd George [Co]	1783 ... William Pitt [The Younger] [T]
1908 .... Herbert Asquith [Li & Co]	1783 .... William Bentinck [T]
1905 .. H. Campbell-Bannerman [Li]	1782 .... William FitzMaurice [W]
1902 .... Arthur Balfour [C]	1782 ..... C. Watson-Wentworth [W]
1895 .... Marquess of Salisbury [C]	1770 .... Frederick North [T]
1894 .... Earl of Rosebery [Li]	1767 .... Augustus Fitzroy [W]
1892 .... William Gladstone [Li]	1766 .... William Pitt [The Elder] [W]
1886 ..... Marquess of Salisbury [C]	1765 ..... C. Watson-Wentworth [W]
1886 ...... William Gladstone [Li]	1763 .... George Grenville [W]
1885 ...... Marquess of Salisbury [C]	1762 .... John Stuart [T]
1880 .... William Gladstone [Li]	1757 .... T. Pelham-Holles [W]
1874 .... Benjamin Disraeli [C]	1756 .... William Cavendish [W]
1868 .... William Gladstone [Li]	1754 .... T. Pelham-Holles [W]
1868 .... Benjamin Disraeli [C]	1743 .... Henry Pelham [W]
1866 .... Edward Stanley [C]	1742 .... Spencer Compton [W]
1865 .... John Russell [Li]	1721 .... Sir Robert Walpole [W]

[W]hig · [Li]beral · [T]ory · [L]abour · [C]onservative · [N]ational · [Co]alition

The term *Prime Minister* was initially one of abuse, with the position referred to formally as *First Lord of the Treasury*. It was only in 1905 that *'Prime Minister'* was used in a Royal Warrant; the first Act of Parliament to refer directly to the *Prime Minister* was the Chequers Estate Act 1917.

───────────── BRITISH PASSPORT WORDING ─────────────

'Her Britannic Majesty's Principal Secretary of State for Foreign and Commonwealth Affairs requests and requires in the name of Her Majesty all those whom it may concern to allow the bearer to pass freely without let or hindrance and to afford the bearer such assistance and protection as may be necessary.'

───────────── SOME FOOTBALL TEAMS ─────────────

Nickname	Team	Home Ground
Gunners	Arsenal	Highbury
Villains	Aston Villa	Villa Park
Rovers	Blackburn Rovers	Ewood Park
Trotters, Wanderers	Bolton Wanderers	Reebok Stadium
Addicks	Charlton Athletic	The Valley
Blues	Chelsea	Stamford Bridge
Rams	Derby County	Pride Park
Toffees	Everton	Goodison Park
Cottagers	Fulham	Craven Cottage
Blues	Ipswich Town	Portman Road
Whites, United	Leeds United	Elland Road
Foxes	Leicester City	Filbert Street
Reds	Liverpool	Anfield
Red Devils	Manchester United	Old Trafford
Boro	Middlesbrough	Riverside Stadium
Magpies	Newcastle United	St James's Park
Saints	Southampton	St Mary's Stadium
Black Cats	Sunderland	Stadium of Light
Spurs	Tottenham Hotspur	White Hart Lane
Hammers	West Ham United	Boleyn Ground
Hornets	Watford	Vicarage Road

───────────── WINDS ─────────────

There are many systems of nomenclature for the naming of winds; they vary by location, language, and tradition. One of the systems which is often seen around the edges of old maps is based on the following names:

Tramontana	Northerly		Ostro	Southerly
Greco	North-easterly		Libeccio	South-westerly
Levante	Easterly		Ponente	Westerly
Sirocco	South-easterly		Maestro	North-westerly

─────────────── BOOKS OF THE BIBLE ───────────────

Old Testament · Genesis · Exodus · Leviticus · Numbers · Deuteronomy
Joshua · Judges · Ruth · First Book of Samuel · Second Book of Samuel
First Book of Kings · Second Book of Kings · First Book of Chronicles
Second Book of Chronicles · Ezra · Nehemiah · Esther · Job · Psalms
Proverbs · Ecclesiastes · The Song of Songs, Song of Solomon, Canticles
Isaiah · Jeremiah · Lamentations · Ezekiel · Daniel · Hosea · Joel · Amos
Obadiah · Jonah · Micah · Nahum · Habakkuk · Zephaniah · Haggai
Zechariah · Malachi · *New Testament* · Gospel According to St Matthew
Gospel According to St Mark · Gospel According to St Luke · Gospel
According to St John · Acts of the Apostles · Epistle to the Romans · First
Epistle to the Corinthians · Second Epistle to the Corinthians · Epistle to
the Galatians · Epistle to the Ephesians · Epistle to the Philippians
Epistle to the Colossians · First Epistle to the Thessalonians · Second
Epistle to the Thessalonians · First Epistle to Timothy · Second Epistle to
Timothy · Epistle to Titus · Epistle to Philemon · Epistle to the Hebrews
Epistle of James · First Epistle of Peter · Second Epistle of Peter · First
Epistle of John · Second Epistle of John · Third Epistle of John · Epistle
of Jude · Revelation, Apocalypse · *Apocrypha* · The First Book of Esdras
The Second Book of Esdras · Tobit · Judith · Rest of Esther · The Wisdom
of Solomon · Ecclesiasticus, Wisdom of Jesus the Son of Sirach · Baruch
Song of the Three Children · Susanna · Bel and the Dragon · Prayer of
Manasses · First Book of the Maccabees · Second Book of the Maccabees

─────────────── SOME PRIME NUMBERS ───────────────

2	61	149	239	347	443	563	659	773	887
3	67	151	241	349	449	569	661	787	907
5	71	157	251	353	457	571	673	797	911
7	73	163	257	359	461	577	677	809	919
11	79	167	263	367	463	587	683	811	929
13	83	173	269	373	467	593	691	821	937
17	89	179	271	379	479	599	701	823	941
19	97	181	277	383	487	601	709	827	947
23	101	191	281	389	491	607	719	829	953
29	103	193	283	397	499	613	727	839	967
31	107	197	293	401	503	617	733	853	971
37	109	199	307	409	509	619	739	857	977
41	113	211	311	419	521	631	743	859	983
43	127	223	313	421	523	641	751	863	991
47	131	227	317	431	541	643	757	877	997
53	137	229	331	433	547	647	761	881	1009
59	139	233	337	439	557	653	769	883	1013

SPECIFICATIONS OF THE EARTH

Equatorial diameter.. 7,926.381m	Surface gravity.......... 980 cm/s²
Polar diameter 7,899.806m	Escape velocity...... 11.18 km/s²
Volume 259,875,300,000m³	Planet Year.......... 365.256 days
Mass............... 5.974 x 10²⁷g	Core temperature..... 4500ºC (est)
Age........ c.4,500,000,000 years	Water:land ratio ...71%:29% (est)

FAMOUS LAST WORDS

RUDOLPH VALENTINO
Don't pull down the blinds!
I feel fine.
I want the sunlight to greet me.

EDVARD GRIEG
Well, if it must be so.

ARNOLD BENNETT
Everything has gone wrong, my girl.

JANE AUSTEN
[is there anything you require?]
Nothing but death.

DYLAN THOMAS
I've had eighteen straight whiskies,
I think that's a record.

BENJAMIN DISRAELI
I am not afraid to die.

GUSTAV MAHLER
Mozart!

CHARLES FOSTER KANE
Rosebud.

OSCAR WILDE
Either that wallpaper goes, or I do.

NOËL COWARD
Good night, my darlings, I'll see
you in the morning.

BLAISE PASCAL
May God never abandon me.

J.M. TURNER
The sun is God.

IMMANUEL KANT
It is enough.

WINSTON CHURCHILL
Oh, I am so bored with it all.

JAMES JOYCE
Does nobody understand?

THE CHATHAM HOUSE RULE

In order to encourage free and open debate on sensitive political issues, the Royal Institute of International Affairs, in 1927, devised the Chatham House Rule. Named after the Institute's London HQ, the Rule is a morally binding convention which allows all or part of a meeting to be held 'off the record'. Information gleaned under the Chatham House Rule may be reported, but the identity or affiliations of speakers must not be disclosed.

MORSE CODE

A	· —	A	M	— —	M	Y	— · — —	Y
B	— · · ·	B	N	— ·	N	Z	— — · ·	Z
C	— · — ·	C	O	— — —	O	0	— — — — —	0
D	— · ·	D	P	· — — ·	P	1	· — — — —	1
E	·	E	Q	— — · —	Q	2	· · — — —	2
F	· · — ·	F	R	· — ·	R	3	· · · — —	3
G	— — ·	G	S	· · ·	S	4	· · · · —	4
H	· · · ·	H	T	—	T	5	· · · · ·	5
I	· ·	I	U	· · —	U	6	— · · · ·	6
J	· — — —	J	V	· · · —	V	7	— — · · ·	7
K	— · —	K	W	· — —	W	8	— — — · ·	8
L	· — · ·	L	X	— · · —	X	9	— — — — ·	9

OFT CONFUSED WORDS

The CAPITOL building .... is situated in the CAPITAL city
The STATUE had such STATURE ...... there was a STATUTE to protect it
Members of the COUNCIL ...... mocked the lawyers for their COUNSEL
It is my guiding TENET ...., to overcharge my TENANTS
Each business was a DISCRETE entity........ so we had to be DISCREET
A judge should be DISINTERESTED.......... but never UNINTERESTED
The arrival of the EMINENT scientist..... was thought to be IMMINENT
I tried to AFFECT the jury's decision .... the EFFECT of which was a fine
They FLAUNTED the fact .... that they FLOUTED the law
I was asked to FORWARD .... the new FOREWORD I had written
One should be WARY............................ of driving when WEARY
Due to the RAIN throughout her REIGN..... the Queen grips her REINS
After FLOUNDERING about......... he FOUNDERED beneath the waves
I took a PEEK at the mountain PEAK... which had PIQUED my curiosity
The school PRINCIPAL.................... is a woman of few PRINCIPLES
The vehicle delivering STATIONERY........., was STATIONARY in traffic
The COMPLIMENTARY wine........ COMPLEMENTED the fish perfectly
I will ACCEPT all gifts .... EXCEPT those that are cheap
The police could not ELICIT a confession.... about his ILLICIT activities
The STRAIT of Hormuz............................ is far from STRAIGHT
There was an ORDINANCE .... against firing any ORDNANCE
He was TAUGHT not to TAUNT........... the woman for her TAUT grip
Poor weather meant the GUERRILLAS shot.... the GORILLAS in the mist
This FOWL... tastes FOUL
His company was INTOLERABLE....... because he was so INTOLERANT
Hospital PATIENTS .... need to have PATIENCE
Building SITES are splendid SIGHTS ...... so we CITE them in the guide

──── ROUGH CLOTHING CONVERSIONS ────

Men's Shoes						
British	6	7	8	9	10	11
American	7½	8½	9½	10½	11½	12½
European	39½	40½	41½	42½	43½	44½
Women's Shoes						
British	3	4	5	6	7	8
American	4½	5½	6½	7½	8½	9½
European	35	36	37	38	39	40
Women's Clothes						
British	10	12	14	16	18	20
American	8	10	12	14	16	18
French	40	42	44	46	48	50
Italian	44	46	48	50	52	54
German	36	38	40	42	44	46
Men's Suits						
British	34	36	38	40	42	44
American	34	36	38	40	42	44
European	44	46	48	50	52	54

Men's Shirts							
British	14	14½	15	15½	16	16½	17
American	14	14½	15	15½	16	16½	17
European	36	37	38	39	40	41	42
Men's Socks							
British	9½	10	10½	11	11½	12	12½
American	9½	10	10½	11	11½	12	12½
European	38–9	39–40	40–1	41–2	42–3	43–4	44–5

──── POLO CHUKKAS ────

The game of Polo is divided into *chukkas* of seven and a half minutes. At the end of each *chukka* a bell is rung, and the play is extended for thirty seconds unless the ball goes out of play, or the umpire calls a foul. [The last *chukka* of a match stops after seven minutes with no additional time added.] Between each *chukka* there is a three-minute interval – extended to five minutes at half-time. A full match lasts for six *chukkas*, but sometimes four or eight are played by mutual agreement. If, at the end of the final *chukka*, the scores are tied, then an interval of five minutes is called, the distance between the goals is widened from eight to sixteen yards, and additional *chukkas* are played until the deciding goal is scored.

[*The* Oxford English Dictionary *gives the etymology of* chukka *as derived from the Hindustani* chakar *and the Sanskrit* cakra *meaning circle or wheel.*]

—— COMMONPLACE FRENCH ——

agent provocateur . . . . one who incites another
amour-propre . . . . self-esteem, self-love; sometimes vanity
ancien régime . . . . the old regime; the regime before the present state
au fond . . . . fundamentally
beau geste . . . . a gesture of magnanimity
belle époque . . . . a golden age; in France, that preceding WWI
chacun à son goût . . . . to each his own taste
comme il faut . . . . correct; appropriate and fitting
de rigueur . . . . absolutely required (by social convention)
éminence grise . . . . the power behind the throne
faute de mieux . . . . for the lack of any better alternative
fin de siècle . . . . the end of the (nineteenth) century; decadent, louche
haut monde . . . . fashionable society
idée fixe . . . . an obsession
lèse-majesté . . . . an offence against the Sovereign
noblesse oblige . . . . the obligations imposed by rank and privilege
raison d'être . . . . the reason for existence
touché . . . . acknowledgement of a point scored in argument
trompe l'oeil . . . . painting style which deceives the eye

—— LINNAEAN ORDER OF CLASSIFICATION ——

KINGDOM
subkingdom
PHYLUM
subphylum
superclass
CLASS
subclass
infraclass
cohort
superorder
ORDER
suborder
superfamily
FAMILY
subfamily
tribe
GENUS
subgenus
SPECIES
subspecies

USEFUL WORDS FOR WORD GAMES

aa
aas
aat

aba – Sack-like garment

abb
aby
ach
act
ad
ado
ads
adz
ae
aft
aga
ah
aha
ahs

ai – S. American 3-toed sloth

aia
ail
ain
ais
ake
ala
alb
alp
als
alt
ami
ana
ane
ani
ann
ar
arb
ard
ars
ary

auf
auk
ava
ave
aw
awa
awn
ax
ay
ays
ayu
ba
baa
bah
bam
bel
ben
bey
bez
bi
bio
bis
biz
bo
boa
bod
boh
bok
bon
bop
bor
bos
bot
bow
bro
brrr
bub

bur
bys
cam
caw
cay
cee
cel
cep
ch
cha
che
chi
cid
cig
cit
cly
col
con
coo
cop
cor
cos
coz
cru
cud
cuz
cwm
cwms
da
dae
dag
dah
dak
dal
dan
dap
das

daw
deb
dee
def
dei
del
dey
di
dib
dit
div
do
dob
doc
dod
doh
doo
dop
dor
dos
dow
dso
dub
dun
duo
dup
dux
dzo
ea
ean
eas
eau
ech
eco
ecu
edh
ee

eek
een
ef
eff
efs
eft
ehs

eik – Greasing liniment

el
eld
ell
els
elt
eme
emu
ene
eng
ere
erf
erg
erk
ern
err
ers
es
ess
est
eta
eth
euk
euoi
euoua
ewk
ewt
ex
fa
fah
fap
fas
faw
fet

feu
fey
fid
fil
fir
fiz
flysch

foh
fon
fou
foy
fra
fro
fub
fud
fug
fum
fy
gad
gae
gal
gam
gan
gar
gat
gau
ged
gee
gen
geu
gey
ghi
ghyll
ghylls
gi
gib
gid
gie
gif
gio

gip
gis
git
gju
glyph
glyphs
gnu

goa
goe
gon
goo
gos
gov
goy
gu
gub
gue
gup
gur
gus
guv
guy
gymp
gymps
gyny
gyp
gyppy
gyps
hae
hah
haj
han
hap
haw
hep
hes
het
hew
hex
hic

hie
hin
ho
hoa
hoc
hod
hoh
hoi
hon
hoo
hos
hox
hoy
htmn
hub
hue
hug
huh
hui
hup
hut
hwyl
hwyls
hye

hyp – Hypochondria

hyps
ich
id
ide
ids
iff
ifs
ins
io
ion
ios
ish
ism
iso
ita
jag

jak
jap
jar
jee
jeu
jiz
jo
jor
jow
jud
jus
ka
kae
kai
kam
kas
kat
kaw
kay
kea
keb
ked
kef
keg
ken
kep
ket
kex
key
kif
kir
ko
koa
kob
kon
kop
kos
kow
ky
kye

kyu
la
lac
lah
lam
lar
las
lat
lav
law
lea
led
lee
lei
lek
lep
les
leu
lev
lew
lex
ley
lez
li
lib
lig
lin
lip
lis
lit
lor
los
lox
loy
lud
lug
lum
lur
luv
lux

——— USEFUL WORDS cont. ———

luz	na	oda	pap	rah	san	sylph	tyg	wat	yok
lye	nab	ods	par	raj	sar	sylphs	tymp	waw	yon
lym	nae	oe	pas	ras	saz	synd	tynd	wem	yos
lyms	nam	oes	pax	rax	scry	synds	udo	wcn	yow
ma	nan	oh	pec	ray	sec	syzygy	uds	wex	yu
maa	nas	oho	ped	re	sed	ta	uey	wey	yug
mac	nat	oi	ph	rec	seg	tae	ufo	wha	yuk
mae	ne	oke	phi	ree	sei	tai			
mag	neb	ole	pho	ref	sel	taj			

ug – *Fear or dread* (definition box)

mak	ned	olm	phs	reh	sen	tak			
mal	nee	om	pi	rem	set	tam	ugh	wis	yup
mar	nef	oms	pia	ren	sez	tau	ugs	wo	yus
mas	nek	ons	pic	rep	sh	taw	uke	wok	zap
maw	nep	oo	pir	res	si	tay	uli	won	zax
max	nid	oof	piu	ret	sib	te	um	wop	zea
meg	nie	ooh	pix	rev	sic	ted	un	wos	zed
mel	nil	oom	po	rcw	sim	tef	uni	wot	zee
mes	nim	oon	poa	rex	ska	teg	uns	wox	zek
meu	nis	oop	poh	rez	sma	tel	ups	wud	zel
mew	nix	oor	poi	rho	sny	ten	ur	wns	zex
mho	noh	oos	pom	rhy	soc	tes	urd	wye	zho
mi	nom	ope	pos	ria	sog	tew	ure	wyn	zig
mil	nos	orc	pow	rin	soh	thymy	ut	wynd	ziz
				rit	sol	ti	ute	wynds	zo

mim – *Modest and demure* (definition box)

				riz	son	tid	uts	wynn	zoa
				rob	sos	tig	utu	wynns	zos
mir	nox	ord	poz	roc	sot	til	uva	wyns	zuz
miz	noy	orf	pre	rok	sou	tim	vac	xi	
mna	nth	ors	prys	rom	sov	toc	vae	xis	
mo	nu	ort	psi	roo	sox	tod	van	xu	
moa	nur	os	psst	ruc	st	tor	vas	xylyl	
moe	nus	ou	pst	rud	sub	tryp	van	xylyls	
mog	ny	ouk	puh	rya	sui	tryps	vee	xyst	
moi	nye	oup	pur	rynd	suk	tui	vid	xysts	
mon	nys	ova	pye	rynds	sup	tum	vin	yah	
mor	ob	ow	pyx	sab	sur	tut	vly	yaw	
mot	oba	owt	qat	sae		tux	voe	yep	
mou	obi	oy					vol	yew	
moy	obo	oye					vor	yex	
mu	obs	oys					vug	ygo	

qi – *A vital force in Taoism* (definition box)

mun	oca	pa	qis	sai	sus	twa	vum	yin	
mus	och	pah	qua	sal	swy	twp	wae	yo	
mux	od	pam	rad	sam	sye	tye	wap	yod	

Most obvious words have been omitted

— 129 —

—— LONDON TELEPHONE EXCHANGE CODES ——

Before the recent revolution in communication technology, London telephone exchanges were identified by a three-character alphanumeric code. For example, a number which started 629 will have been served by the MAYfair exchange (M=6, A=2, Y=9). Most exchanges were named after their geographical locations; however, some had abstract names, and others were named after local shops or landmarks (TATe Gallery 828, LORds 507, or MUSeum 687, for example). The following table shows some of the London exchange codes which were still in use *circa* 1968.

Old	Exchange	New Code	Area served
206	CONcord	864	South Harrow
208	COVent Garden	240	Covent Garden
222	ABBey	222	Westminster
235	BELgravia	235	Belgravia
247	BIShopsgate	247	City of London
278	BRUnswick	278	King's Cross
353	FLEet Street	353	Fleet Street
426	HAMpstead	435	Hampstead
437	GERrard	437	Soho
470	GROsvenor	499	Mayfair
485	GULliver	485	Kentish Town, Camden
507	LORds	289	Lords and Maida Vale
626	MANsion House	626	City of London
629	MAYfair	629	Mayfair
632	MEAdway	458	Golders Green
687	MUSeum	636	Bloomsbury
723	PADdington	723	Paddington
773	SPEedwell	455	Golders Green
828	TATe Gallery	828	Victoria
944	WHItehall	930	Westminster

[*The famous number for Old Scotland Yard was 'Whitehall 1212', and many police station numbers still end 1212. New Scotland Yard is 020 7230 1212.*]

———————— SOME COMPOUNDS ————————

Testosterone............ $C_{19}H_{28}O_2$	Fool's Gold................... FeS_2
Asbestos .... $CaMg_3(SiO_3)_4$	Limestone................. $CaCO_3$
Aspirin.... $CH_3CO_2C_6H_4COOH$	Nitroglycerin........... $H_5(NO_3)_3$
Vitamin A .... $C_{20}H_{29}OH$	Caffeine.............. $C_8H_{10}O_2N_4$
Clay........... $H_2Al_2(SiO_4)_2 \cdot H_2O$	Gunpowder................. KNO_3
Camphor .... $C_{10}H_{16}O$	Adrenaline .... $C_9H_{13}NO_3$

THE NINE MUSES

CLIO *history* · MELPOMENE *tragedy* · THALIA *comedy*
CALLIOPE *epic poetry* · URANIA *astronomy* · EUTERPE *flutes and music*
TERPSICHORE *dancing and lyric poetry*
POLYHYMNIA *mime and sacred poetry* · ERATO *love poetry*

The Nine Muses are the Greek goddesses of learning, arts, culture, and inspiration. They are the progeny of Zeus and Mnemosyne (memory), and were born in Piera at the foot of Mount Olympus. For centuries the Muses have been worshipped and venerated for their patronage of music, art, drama, and poetry – not least by Plato, Aristotle, and Ptolemy I. Traditionally, those places dedicated to the greater glory of the Nine Muses were known as *mouseion*, from which we derive the word *museum*.

SOME MUSICAL TERMINOLOGY

Adagio	slow
Affrettando	hurrying onwards
Agitati	agitated
Allargando	getting slower
Allegro	fast, lively
Andante	walking pace
Animato	animated
Appassionato	passionately
Arpeggiare	like a harp
Bravura	boldness and spirit
Brio	vigour
Con anima	with feeling
Deciso	decisively, firmly
Dolce	sweetly, tenderly
Dolcissimo	very sweetly & gently
Dolente	sadly
Energico	with energy
Forte-piano	loud, then soft
Forzando	sudden emphasis
Fugato	in fugal style
Grave	slow and solemn
Impetuoso	impetuously
Lacrimoso	sadly, tearfully
Largo	slow and stately
Legato	smoothly
Leggiero	nimble and delicate
L'istesso tempo	maintain speed
Lontano	as from a distance
Lusingando	caressingly
Ma non troppo	but not too much
Mancando	dying away
Martellato	hammered out
Morendo	slowly dying away
Nobilmente	nobly
Parlante	sung as spoken
Passionato	passionately
Patètico	with great feeling
Piacevole	agreeably
Pizzicato	plucked, picked
Prestissimo	as fast as possible
Rallentando	gradually slower
Rigoroso	strictly, rigorous
Risvegliato	increasingly animated
Ritardando	gradually held back
Scherzando	playful
Slargando	gradually slower
Smorzando	dying away
Staccato	detached
Strepitoso	boisterously
Suave	gentle, smooth
Tacet	silent
Tempo primo	at original speed
Teneramente	tenderly
Tranquillo	calmly

———— UK CHRISTMAS NUMBER 1 SINGLES ————

1969 *Two Little Boys*..Rolf Harris
1970 *I Hear You Knocking*............................Dave Edmunds
1971 *Ernie (The Fastest Milkman In The West)*..............Benny Hill
1972 *Long Haired Lover From Liverpool*..........Little Jimmy Osmond
1973 *Merry Xmas Everybody* ....Slade
1974 *Lonely This Christmas*...Mud
1975 *Bohemian Rhapsody*..Queen
1976 *When A Child Is Born (Soleado)*....................Johnny Mathis
1977 *Mull Of Kintyre / Girls' School* ....Wings
1978 *Mary's Boy Child / Oh My Lord*..........................Boney M
1979 *Another Brick In The Wall (Part II)*......................Pink Floyd
1980 *There's No-One Quite Like Grandma* ... St Winifred's School Choir
1981 *Don't You Want Me?*..............................Human League
1982 *Save Your Love*...............................Renée and Renato
1983 *Only You*..Flying Pickets
1984 *Do They Know It's Christmas?*............................Band Aid
1985 *Merry Christmas Everyone*.....................Shakin' Stevens
1986 *Reet Petite*...Jackie Wilson
1987 *Always On My Mind*.............................Pet Shop Boys
1988 *Mistletoe And Wine* ....Cliff Richard
1989 *Do They Know It's Christmas?*.........................Band Aid II
1990 *Saviour's Day*...Cliff Richard
1991 *Bohemian Rhapsody*..Queen
1992 *I Will Always Love You*.......................Whitney Houston
1993 *Mr Blobby*...Mr Blobby
1994 *Stay Another Day* ....East 17
1995 *Earth Song*..Michael Jackson
1996 *2 Become 1*..Spice Girls
1997 *Too Much*..Spice Girls
1998 *Goodbye*..Spice Girls
1999 *I Have A Dream / Seasons In The Sun*......................Westlife
2000 *Can We Fix It?*.....................................Bob the Builder
2001 *Somethin' Stupid*...............Robbie Williams & Nicole Kidman

———— TEMPERATURE CONVERSION ————

To convert º Celsius to º Fahrenheit........ multiply by 1.8 and add 32
To convert º Fahrenheit to º Celsius....... subtract 32 and divide by 1.8

Rule-of-Thumb Approximate Reversible Temperatures
16 º Centigrade = 61 º Fahrenheit
28 º Centigrade = 82 º Fahrenheit

KNITTING ABBREVIATIONS

*	indicates a repeat
approx.	approximately
b	in back of stitch; bobble
beg	beginning
bh	button hole
bo	bind off; body gauge
col	colour
con; cc	contrasting colour
con	cast on
cont	continue
dtr	double treble crochet
e	every
ea	each
e(o)r	every (other) row
est	established
fol	following
g-st	garter stitch
kssb	knit slip stitch through back
m	make
mc	main colour
mr	mark row
ms	mark stitch
odl	or desired length
p	purl
pat	pattern

pfc	present for Christmas
psso	pass slipped stitch(es) over
pu	pick up
r(h)	right (hand)
rem	remaining
rep	repeat
req	required
rev	reverse
rnd	round
rs	right side
selv	selvedge
sk	skein
skp	slip, knit, psso
sl	slip
ssk	slip, slip, knit 2 tog
st(s)	stitch(es)
st st	stockinette stitch
tbl	through the back loop
tfl	through the front loop
tog	together
ws	wrong side
x	times
yb	yarn back
yf	yarn forward
yo	yarn over

ABRACADABRA

The word employed by so many second-rate conjurers has long had associations with magic and superstition. The first written example of *abracadabra* is thought to be in the poem *Praecepta de Medicina*, by the writer Q. Severus Sammonicus in the second century. When written in the triangular form shown opposite, and when worn around the neck, *abracadabra* was considered to have healing powers, perhaps

```
A B R A C A D A B R A
 A B R A C A D A B R
  A B R A C A D A B
   A B R A C A D A
    A B R A C A D
     A B R A C A
      A B R A C
       A B R A
        A B R
         A B
          A
```

because it repeated the letters ABRA – a possible reference to the Hebrew words signifying Father, Son, and Holy Spirit: *Ab, Ben* & *Rauch Acadosh*.

CHILTERN HUNDREDS

As the result of a curious resolution passed by the House of Commons in 1623, MPs are unable to simply resign. Seats can only be vacated by: an MP's death; elevation to the peerage; disqualification; expulsion; or by the dissolution of Parliament. Thus, an MP who wishes to leave the House of Commons is obliged to engineer disqualification by applying for a spurious, paid office of the Crown. Traditionally, the two offices are:

Crown Steward and Bailiff of the three
Chiltern Hundreds of Stoke, Desborough, and Burnham
and
The Manor of Northstead

Once an MP has applied for one of these posts, his Warrant of Office is signed by the Chancellor of the Exchequer, his parliamentary seat becomes vacant, and a by-election writ is moved in the usual way. A few who have recently left Parliament invoking this antique methodology are:

Betty Boothroyd [C100s] · Alastair Goodlad [C100s] · Neil Kinnock [C100s]
Leon Brittan [MoN] · Matthew Parris [MoN] · J. Enoch Powell [MoN]

LUCASIAN PROFESSORS

The Lucasian *Professorship of Mathematick* was endowed by Henry Lucas, MP for Cambridge University. On his death in December 1663, Lucas bequeathed land in his will to create an annual income of £100 to finance the chair. The Professorship received the ratification of Charles II in 1664.

1664–1669	Isaac Barrow[F]	1826–1828	Sir George Airy[P]
1669–1702	Sir Isaac Newton[P]	1828–1839	Charles Babbage[F]
1702–1710	William Whiston	1839–1849	Joshua King
1711–1739	Nicolas Saunderson[F]	1849–1903	Sir George Stokes[P]
1739–1760	John Colson[F]	1903–1932	Sir Joseph Larmor[V]
1760–1798	Edward Waring[F]	1932–1969	Paul Dirac[F]
1798–1820	Isaac Milner[F]	1969–1980	Sir James Lighthill[V]
1820–1822	Robert Woodhouse[F]	1980–	Stephen Hawking[F]
1822–1826	Thomas Turton	Royal Society: [P]resident · [V]ice-President · [F]ellow	

ADULT DENTITION

After the age of six or so, the 'milk-teeth' are replaced by 32 adult teeth:
8 incisors · 4 canines · 8 pre-molars · 12 molars (2 being 'wisdom teeth')

—MURDER METHODS IN MISS MARPLE NOVELS—

The following chart tabulates some of the murder techniques employed in the *Miss Marple* novels of Dame Agatha Christie. It excludes the short stories.

	gunshot	burning	head wound	strangling	falling	poison		
Murder at the Vicarage	▪							1930
The Body in the Library		▪	▪			▪		1942
The Moving Finger			▪			▪		1943
A Murder is Announced	▪			▪				1950
They Do It With Mirrors	▪	▪						1952
A Pocket Full of Rye				▪		▪		1953
4.50 From Paddington				▪				1957
The Mirror Crack'd From Side to Side	▪					▪		1962
A Caribbean Mystery						▪		1964
At Bertram's Hotel	▪							1965
Nemesis				▪	▪	▪		1971
Sleeping Murder				▪				1976

—COLOUR SPECTRUM & MNEMONIC—

R*ichard* O*f* Y*ork* G*ave* B*attle* I*n* V*ain*
R*ed*   O*range* Y*ellow* G*reen* B*lue* I*ndigo* V*iolet*

—CASTRATI—

The Castrato voice (created by the removal of the testes of a young choirboy) was either soprano or alto, and it developed as the Castrato matured. Though never officially sanctioned by the Church, the practice of castration lasted in Europe from the mid C16th until the 1870s. Famous Castrati include: SENESINO (*c.*1680–1759); FARINELLI (1705–82); MANZUOLI (1725–82); and the 'last castrato' MORESCHI (1858–1922), who entered the Sistine Chapel in 1883, and became conductor of the choir in 1898. Moreschi made seventeen recordings before he retired in 1913.

—A FEW ANGLO-INDIAN WORDS—

Pukka	first rate	*Chotta*	small
Chitty	letter, note or pass	*Pani*	water
Khak	dust (hence khaki)	*Sub chiz*	everything
Kutcha	opposite of *pukka*	*Jharan*	cloth, duster
Wallah	person, usually worker	*Peg*	a measure of drink

METRIC WIRE GAUGES

The following table gives the metric equivalents for the British Standard Wire Gauge (SWG). Readers familiar with wire gauges will not need reminding of the importance of distinguishing between SWG and the other wire-gauges including: American Wire Gauge (AWG) [also known as Brown & Sharpe]; Birmingham Sheet & Hoop; Stubs; Stubs Steel; Stubs Iron (Birmingham Gauge); US standard plate; and Washburn & Moen.

STANDARD WIRE GAUGE	DIAMETER OF WIRE							
	inch	cm						
0	.324	.823	15	.072	.183	33	.0100	.0254
1	.300	.762	16	.064	.163	34	.0092	.0234
2	.276	.701	17	.056	.142	35	.0084	.0213
3	.252	.640	18	.048	.122	36	.0076	.0193
4	.232	.589	19	.040	.102	37	.0068	.0173
5	.212	.538	20	.036	.0914	38	.0060	.0152
6	.192	.488	21	.032	.0813	39	.0052	.0132
7	.176	.447	22	.028	.0711	40	.0048	.0122
8	.160	.406	23	.024	.0610	41	.0044	.0112
9	.144	.366	24	.022	.0559	42	.0040	.0102
10	.128	.325	25	.020	.0508	43	.0036	.0091
11	.116	.295	26	.018	.0457	44	.0032	.0081
12	.104	.264	27	.0164	.0417	45	.0028	.0071
13	.092	.234	28	.0149	.0378	46	.0024	.0061
14	.080	.203	29	.0136	.0345	47	.0020	.0051
			30	.0124	.0315	48	.0016	.0041
			31	.0116	.0295	49	.0012	.0030
			32	.0108	.0274	50	.0010	.0025

MAGPIES

Magpies have been the subject of folklore and superstition in cultures across the world. Celtic lore associated magpies with Christianity; Norse myth, with sexual union; Roman myth, with the sensual pleasures of Bacchus; and Chinese myth, with marital bliss. English folklore has long associated magpies with the following rhyme; and although a number of historic versions and regional variations of this rhyme exist, it seems universally held that a lone magpie is an omen of impending bad luck.

One for sorrow, Two for joy, Three for a girl, Four for a boy,
Five for silver, Six for gold, Seven for a secret as yet untold.

One for sorrow, Two for mirth, Three for a wedding
Four for a birth, Five for a christening, Six for a dearth,
Seven for heaven, Eight for hell, Nine for the Devil himself.

———— HUNTING OPEN SEASONS ————

Season Starts	GAME BIRDS AND WILDFOWL	Season Ends
12 August	Grouse	10 December
12 August	Ptarmigan	10 December
20 August	Black Game	10 December
1 September	Partridge	1 February
1 October	Pheasant	1 February
1 October	Capercaillie	31 January
12 August	Snipe	31 January
1 September	Woodcock (Scotland)	31 January
1 October	Woodcock (England & Wales)	31 January
1 September	Wild Duck & Geese (Inland)	31 January
1 September	Wild Duck & Geese (below high-water mark)	20 February

Scotland	DEER	England & Wales
1 Jul – 20 Oct	Red Stags	1 Aug – 30 Apr
21 Oct – 15 Feb	Red Hinds	1 Nov – 28/9 Feb
1 Aug – 30 Mar	Fallow Buck	1 Aug – 30 Apr
21 Oct – 15 Feb	Fallow Doe	1 Nov – 28/9 Feb
1 May – 20 Oct	Roe Buck	1 Apr – 31 Oct
21 Oct – 28/9 Feb	Roe Doe	1 Nov – 28/9 Feb
1 Aug – 30 Apr	Sika Stags	1 Aug – 30 Apr
21 Oct – 15 Feb	Sika Hinds	1 Nov – 28/9 Feb

Most hunting is either prohibited or frowned upon on Christmas Day.

———— PRE-DECIMAL BRITISH CURRENCY ————

1 guinea	1gn · 1g · £1 1s 0d	21 shillings
1 pound	£1 · £1 0s 0d	20 shillings
1 shilling	1s · 1s 0d · 1/–	12 pence
1 penny	1d	2 halfpennies
1 halfpenny	½d	2 farthings
1 farthing	¼d · far. · f.	

———— GREENELAND ————

The term 'Greeneland' was coined by critic Arthur Calder-Marshall to describe the seedy, introspective, decadent, and curious world portrayed in many of Graham Greene's novels – especially those set in classic Greene territory: *A Burnt Out Case*, Zaire; *The Comedians*, Haiti; *Journey Without Maps*, Liberia; *Brighton Rock*, Brighton gangs; *Our Man in Havana*, Cuba.

ANATOLE'S DISHES

Anatole is the famous gourmet chef at Brinkley Court, the home of Bertie Wooster's favourite uncle and aunt: Tom and Dahlia Travers. Anatole's culinary creations are legendary, and the threat of never tasting them again is usually enough to induce Bertie to do his Aunt's bidding in some burglarious enterprise. Scattered through the Jeeves & Wooster novels of P.G. Wodehouse, a few of these glorious dishes are tabulated below:

Velouté aux fleurs de courgette · Sylphides à la crème d'Ecrivisses
Mignonette de poulet petit duc · Niege aux perles des Alpes
Timbale de ris de veau Toulousaine · Points d'asperges à la Mistinguette
Nonettes de poulet Agnès Sorel · Selle d'Agneau aux laitures à la Grecque
Diablotins · Caviar Frais · Benedictins Blancs

THE METALS OF ALCHEMY

Alchemy is the transmutation of base elements into precious metals such as silver and gold. The process has fascinated philosophers, scientists, clerics, and astrologers throughout time and across cultures. The metals usually linked with this (so far) fruitless search are shown below, along with the planets and deities that they are most commonly associated with.

GOLD *Apollo, the Sun* · SILVER *Diana, the Moon* · TIN *Jupiter*
QUICKSILVER *Mercury* · COPPER *Venus* · IRON *Mars* · LEAD *Saturn*

CLASSIFICATION OF ICEBERG SIZE

HEIGHT *metres above water*	NAME	LENGTH *metres*
<1	GROWLER	<5
1–4	BERGY BIT	5–14
5–15	SMALL	15–60
16–45	MEDIUM	61–120
46–75	LARGE	121–200
>75	VERY LARGE	>200

[The 'tip of the iceberg' is usually thought to be around 1/5th to 1/7th of its total size.]

GULLIVER'S TRAVELS

Lemuel Gulliver voyaged to Lilliput, Brobdingnag, Laputa, Balnibarbi, Luggnagg, Glubbdubdrib, Japan, and to the Land of the Houyhnhnms.

—SESQUIPEDALIAN—

Commonly cited as the longest word in English, the 1,185-character-long name for *Tobacco Mosaic Virus, Dahlemense Stain,* in all its absurdity, is:

*Acetylseryltyrosylsery
lisoleucylthreonylserylprolylserylg
lutaminylphenylalanylvalylphenylalanylle
ucylserylserylvalyltryptophylalanylaspartylprolyl
isoleucylglutamylleucylleucylasparaginylvalylcysteinyl
threonylserylserylleucylglycylasparaginylglutaminylphenyl
alanylglutaminylthreonylglutaminylglutaminylalanylarginy
lthreonylthreonylglutaminylvalylglutaminylglutaminylphenyla
lanylserylglutaminylvalyltryptophyllysylprolylphenylalanylprolylg
lutaminylserylthreonylvalylarginylphenylalanylprolylglycylasparty
lvalyltyrosyllysylvalyltyrosylarginyltyrosylasparaginylalanylvalylleu
cylaspartylprolylleucylisoleucylthreonylalanylleucylleucylglycylthreo
nylphenylalanylaspartylthreonylarginylasparaginylarginylisoleucyli
soleucylglutamylvalylglutamylasparaginylglutaminylglutaminylse
rylprolylthreonylthreonylalanylglutamylthreonylleucylaspartylal
anylthreonylarginylarginylvalylaspartylaspartylalanylthreonyl
valylalanylisoleucylarginylserylalanylasparaginylisoleucylas
paraginylleucylvalylasparaginylglutamylleucylvalylargin
ylglycylthreonylglycylleucyltyrosylasparaginylglutam
inylasparaginylthreonylphenylalanylglutamyls
erylmethionylserylglycylleucylvalyltrypt
ophylthreonylserylalanylprolyl
alanylserine*

Other lovely long words include:

Pneumonoultramicroscopicsilicovolcanoconiosis
a disease caused by the inhalation of fine particles

Antitransubstantiationalist
one who doubts the validity of transubstantiation

Floccinaucinihilipilification
the estimation of a thing as worthless

Antidisestablishmentarianism
opposition of those who oppose the link between Church and State

Sesquipedalian is an interesting word in itself. Said to be coined by Horace, it is a term for words so polysyllabic that they seem 'a foot and a half long'.

NATIONAL NEWSPAPER FOUNDING

The Times........ (1785) 1788 [N]	The Observer .... 1791 [G]
The Scotsman..... (1817) 1855 [Pr]	Sunday Times ..... (1821) 1822 [N]
The Guardian ..... (1821) 1959 [G]	News of the World........ 1843 [N]
Daily Telegraph .... 1855 [T]	Sunday People..... (1881) 1972 [Tr]
Financial Times [§] .... 1888 [P]	Sunday Mirror .... (1915) 1963 [Tr]
Daily Star .... (1888) 1978 [No]	Sunday Express[†] .... 1918 [No]
Daily Mail .... 1896 [A]	Sunday Telegraph .... 1961 [T]
Daily Express .... 1900 [No]	Mail on Sunday.......... 1982 [A]
The Mirror............... 1903 [Tr]	Independent on Sunday .. 1990 [I]
The Sun.......... (1911) 1964 [N]	The (Sunday) Business.... 1998 [Pr]
The Independent .... 1986 [I]	*[bracketed dates are for a former title]*

[†] *1st Crossword 1924 · 1st Times crossword 1930 ·* [§] *1893 printed on pink paper*

Current ownership: [N]ews Corporation · [No]rthern & Shell Media · [P]earson
[T]elegraph Group / Hollinger · [A]ssociated Newspapers · [Pr]ess Holdings
[G]uardian Media Group · [I]ndependent News & Media · [Tr]inity Mirror

THE BIG MAC

The ingredients of a McDonald's Big Mac are: *Beef Patties x2* – 100% pure beef patty. No additives, fillers, binders, preservatives, or flavour enhancers. Just pure forequarter and flank. *Big Mac Bun* – Flour, water, sugar, sesame seeds, rapeseed oil, yeast, salt, soya flour. Emulsifier: E472(e) mono- and di-acetyltartaric acid esters of mono- and di-glycerides of fatty acids. Preservative: E282 calcium propionate. Flour treatment agent: E300 ascorbic acid. *Big Mac Sauce* – Water, vegetable oil, gherkins, sugar, vinegar, modified corn starch, egg yolk, spices, fructose, salt. Stabiliser: E415 xanthan gum. Preservative: E202 potassium sorbate. Spice extracts. *Processed Cheese Slice* – Vegetarian cheddar cheese, water, butter, milk proteins, natural cheese flavouring. Emulsifying salts: E331 trisodium citrate, E450 diphosphates, E452 polyphosphates. Lactose, salt. Preservative: E200 sorbic acid. Colour: E160(a) carotenes, E160(c) paprika. *Lettuce* – 100% shredded iceberg lettuce. *Dill Pickle Slices* – Cucumber, vinegar. Preservatives: E210 benzoic acid, E327 calcium lactate or E200 sorbic acid and E509 calcium chloride. Spices. *Dehydrated Onions* – 100% dehydrated white onions.

A Big Mac contains the following:	Protein (grams)............... 26.7
Energy (Kjoules)............ 2050	Fat (grams)................... 22.9
Energy (Kcalories) 493	– saturates (grams)........... 9.8
Carbohydrates (grams)....... 44.0	Fibre (grams) 5.3
– sugars (grams)............. 11.6	Sodium (grams) 0.9

———— SOME WEDDING SUPERSTITIONS ————

THE BRIDAL GOWN

White . . . . . . you have chosen right	Blue . . . . you'll always be true
Grey . . . . you'll go far away	Pearl . . . . you'll live in a whirl
Black . . . . you'll wish yourself back	Peach . . . . a love out of reach
Red . . . . . . you'll wish yourself dead	Yellow . . . ashamed of your fellow
Green . . . . ashamed to be seen	Pink . . . . your spirits will sink

THE WEDDING DAY

Monday for health, Tuesday for wealth,
Wednesday best of all,
Thursday for losses, Friday for crosses,
Saturday for no luck at all.

THE WEDDING MONTH

Marry in May, and you'll rue the day.
Marry in Lent, you'll live to repent.

Married when the year is new, he'll be loving, kind, and true,
When February birds do sing, cherise you your wedding ring.
If you wed when March winds blow, joy and sorrow both you'll know.
Marry in April if you can, thus joy for Maiden and for Man.
Marry in the month of May, and you will never rue the day.
Marry when June roses grow, over hills and far you'll go.
Those who in July do wed, must labour hard for daily bread.
Whoever wed in August be, many a fortune is sure to see.
Marry in September's shrine, your living will be rich and fine.
If in October you do marry, love will come but riches tarry.
If you wed in bleak November, only joys will come, remember.
When December snows fall fast, marry and true love will last.

CHANGING YOUR NAME

Change the name, and not the letter,
or you change for worse, and not for better.

———— WORDS WITH ALL THE VOWELS IN ————
ALPHABETICAL ORDER

Abstemious · Abstentious · Arsenious · Caesious · Facetious · Fracedinous

SHIPPING FORECAST AREAS

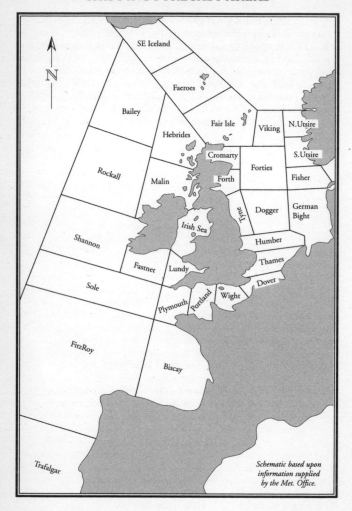

In 2002, the sea-area formerly known as Finisterre was renamed FitzRoy in honour of Captain Robert Fitzroy – the first director of the Met. Office after its creation in 1854. Fitzroy was also captain of HMS *Beagle*, the ship which took Charles Darwin on his 1831 circumnavigation of the globe.

———————————— HRH A.G. CARRICK ————————————

When, in 1987, His Royal Highness, the Prince of Wales submitted one of his watercolours for inclusion in the Royal Academy's annual Summer Exhibition, the painting was entered and accepted under the pseudonym Arthur George Carrick. The painting was signed 'C/87'. The selection of this Royal pseudonym can be explained by examining the Prince of Wales' official title: His Royal Highness Prince Charles Philip Arthur George, Prince of Wales, KG, KT, OM, GCB, AK, QSO, PC, ADC, Earl of Chester, Duke of Cornwall, Duke of Rothesay, Earl of Carrick, Baron of Renfrew, Lord of the Isles and Prince and Great Steward of Scotland.

———————————— TWO DICE ODDS ————————————

number	permutations	odds
12		35/1
11		17/1
10		11/1
9		8/1
8		31/5
7		5/1
6		31/5
5		8/1
4		11/1
3		17/1
2		35/1

——————————— RECTOR OF ST ANDREWS ———————————

The office of Rector of St Andrews University is derived from an Act of 1858, which created the position as the President of the University Court. This rectorship is of particular interest since it is elected by matriculated students, an unusual franchise which may explain the roll-call since 1970:

John Cleese	1970	Stanley Adams	1985
Alan Coren	1973	Nicholas Parsons	1988
Frank Muir[†]	1976	Nicholas Campbell	1991
Tim Brooke-Taylor	1979	Donald Findlay QC	1993
Katharine Whitehorn	1982	Andrew Neil	1999

[†]The University awards the annual Frank Muir Prize for Humour, currently worth £400, to the student who submits the most humorous and witty original composition addressing an aspect of life at St Andrews.

——— SOME BONSAI TREE TERMINOLOGY ———

SOME STYLES		HEIGHT SPECIFICATIONS	
CHOKKAN	formal upright	MAME	< 7 cm
MOYOGI	informal upright	SHOHIN	7–20 cm
KENGAI	cascading form	KIFU	20–40 cm
ISHI SEKI	planted on rock	CHU	40–60 cm
HOKIDACHI	broom-like form	DAI	> 60 cm
SABAMIKI	split trunk		
KABUDACHI	multiple trunks		

[As defined by the 20th Grand View Bonsai Exhibition Nippon Bonsai Taikan-ten.]

——— COFFEE SHOP SLANG ———

Barista	expert espresso maker
Brevé	espresso with semi-skimmed milk
Cake in a Cup	double cream, double sugar
Con Panna	with cream
Crema	dense golden foam found only on good espresso
Demitasse	small espresso cup
Double	two shots of coffee
Double Cupping	two takeaway cups to protect hands
Double Fun	flavouring both coffee and milk
Drip	regular, filter coffee
Dry	foamed (not steamed) milk
Foamless	no foamed milk
Grande	large cup
Granita	Latte with frozen milk
Harmless	Skinny and No Fun
Latte	with milk
Lungo	a long pull of espresso
Macchiato	marked or spotted
No fun	decaffeinated
Quad	four shots of coffee
Short	small cup
Shot in the dark	a cup of Drip, with a shot of espresso
Skinny	semi-skimmed milk
Split	half caff, half decaff
Tall	medium cup
Triple	three shots of coffee
Wet	steamed (not foamed) milk
Whipless	no whipped cream
Wild	with whipped cream
With room	cup not completely filled
With wings	to go

DINING ABOARD THE TITANIC

FIRST CLASS DINNER MENU · 14 APRIL 1912

Hors D'oeuvre Variès · Oysters

Consommé Olga · Cream of Barley

Salmon, Mousseline Sauce, Cucumber

Filet Mignons Lili · Sauté of Chicken, Lyonnaise · Vegetable Marrow Farcie

Lamb, Mint Sauce
Roast Duckling, Apple Sauce
Sirloin of Beef, Chateâu Potatoes

Green Peas · Creamed Carrots · Boiled Rice · Parmentier & New Potatoes

Punch Romaine

Roast Squab & Cress · Cold Asparagus Vinaigrette
Pâté De Foie Gras · Celery

Waldorf Pudding · Peaches in Chartreuse Jelly
Chocolate & Vanilla Eclairs · French Ice Cream

THE TITANIC WAS LOADED WITH THE FOLLOWING PROVISIONS:

Bacon and ham	7,500 lbs	Oranges	80 boxes (36,000)
Coffee	2,200 lbs	Potatoes	40 tons
Flour	200 barrels	Poultry and game	25,000 lbs
Fresh asparagus	800 bundles	Rice, dried beans, &c.	10,000 lbs
Fresh butter	6,000 lbs	Salt and dried fish	4,000 lbs
Fresh cream	1,200 qts	Sausages	2,500 lbs
Fresh eggs	40,000	Sugar	10,000 lbs
Fresh fish	11,000 lbs	Sweetbreads	1,000
Fresh green peas	2,250 lbs	Tea	800 lbs
Fresh meat	75,000 lbs	Cigars	8,000
Fresh milk	1,500 gals	Items of crockery	57,600
Grapefruit	50 boxes	Pieces of cutlery	44,000
Ice Cream	1,750 qts	Pieces of glassware	29,000
Jams and marmalades	1,120 lbs	Beer and stout	20,000 bottles
Lemons	50 boxes (16,000)	Mineral waters	15,000 bottles
Lettuce	7,000 heads	Spirits	850 bottles
Onions	3,500 lbs	Wines	1,500 bottles

BLOOMSBURY

'Bloomsbury' is thought to derive from *Blemondisberi* – the 13th-century manor of William Blemond. The area of London named after it has no formal borders, but is commonly understood to be that enclosed *South* of Euston Road; *North* of New Oxford Street & High Holborn; *East* of Tottenham Court Road; and *West* of Gray's Inn Road. Apart from the British Museum and the University of London, the area is perhaps best known for the 'Bloomsbury Group': a loose association of writers, artists, and academics in the early 1900s. The Group's most notable members included: Leonard and Virginia Woolf, E.M. Forster, Roger Fry, Vanessa and Clive Bell, Lytton Strachey, J.M. Keynes, and Duncan Grant. Predating this famous group was the little known 'Bloomsbury Gang' – an influential Whig faction formed in 1765 by the 4th Duke of Bedford.

LOUIS BRAILLE

An accident in his father's workshop left Louis Braille (1809–52) blind at the age of four. Some seven years later, Braille met Charles Barbier, a soldier who had conceived a 'night writing' code. Realising the potential for communication with the blind, Braille developed a simplified version:

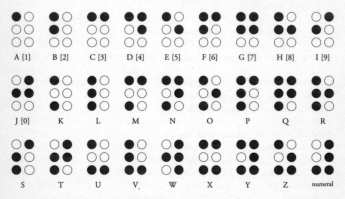

The numeral symbol indicates that the letters A–J are being used as digits.

Braille is based on the above 3x2 dot cells – although other cells exist for punctuation, abbreviations, and so on. A century and a half after Braille's death, his code has been adapted for almost every language, and is in use across the globe. To honour his unique creation, in 1952 Braille's body was moved and re-buried in the Panthéon alongside other French heroes.

—— SOME WORDS FROM OTHER LANGUAGES——

MALAY · Quick! Go and fetch me the ornate *bamboo caddy*, or I will run *amok* in the *compound* wearing nothing but my *gingham sarong*.

ARABIC · The *admiral* in the *alcove*, whilst sitting on his *sequin sofa* dreaming of *harems*, should fear the *assassin* rather than seeking solace in the *alchemy* of *alcohol*.

IRISH GAELIC · Don't give me any more of your *Tory blarney* about the *banshee* wearing *brogues*, or I'll get that *colleen* to smash your *poteen* to *smithereens*.

JAPANESE · Only a *tycoon* or a *mikado* would have a *yen* to recline on his *futon* eating *sushi* with a *geisha*, whilst betting on *judo*.

ALEUT INUIT · My *anorak* is far to cold for a *kayak* expedition to the *igloo*. Bring me that *parka* instead.

FARSI/PERSIAN · This *talc bazaar* has everything! Just one *kiosk* alone sells *lilac tiaras*, and *azure shawls*.

SANSKRIT · The *pundit* and his *guru* were repeating their *mantra*, hoping for *nirvana*, when some fool ruined their *karma*, chipping the *crimson lacquer* on the *chintz*.

TURKISH · Oh! *Effendi!* I really must apologise for spilling *coffee* over your *kilim*, and dripping *yoghurt* over your *turquoise divan*.

CZECH · Fetch the *howitzer!* Some fool's armed the *robot* with a *pistol*.

AFRIKAANS · The *commandos* love nothing more than to *trek* across the *veldt* in search of *wildebeest*.

SWEDISH · The *ombudsman* was dazzled by the harsh *tungsten* light.

WELSH · Wrap that *corgi* in *flannel* and hide him in the *coracle*.

PORTUGUESE · All this *palaver* simply because the *albino albatross* doesn't have a taste for *marmalade*.

NORWEGIAN · It was an error to let the *lemming ski* in the *slalom*.

HUNGARIAN · Get the *sabre* from the *coach!* The *hussar* has overdone the *paprika* and ruined my *goulash*.

ICELANDIC · A *saga* about a *geyser?*

SCOTTISH GAELIC · 'Toss the *caber* from the *glen* over the *loch*' is an absurd *slogan* if all you want to do is sell *plaid trousers* to tourists.

TAGALOG · Look over there. Is that a *ylang-ylang* in the *boondock?*

AZTEC · I'm not eating *avocado* with *chilli* sauce, or *tomato* with *chocolate*. Feed it all to the *coyote!*

RUSSIAN · The *commissar* orders a *mammoth samovar* of *vodka* to be dispatched to the *balalaika* player.

NORSE · *Balderdash, you oaf!* I am so *angry*. If I get an *inkling* you are *flaunting* the *dregs* of your talent, I will cover your *vole* in *glitter*.

—————————— COURT JESTERS ——————————

Dr Doran, in his 1850 *The History of Court Fools,* gives an utterly exhaustive account of licensed and unlicensed court fools, jesters, and mirthmen throughout the ages. The following list is a very brief selection:

ADELSBURN...Jester to George I
'CARDINAL' SOGLIA..........................Jester to Pope Gregory XVI
MERRY ANDREW ....Physician to Henry VIII, and unlicensed fool
ABGELY ....Fool to Louis XIV; the last licensed fool in France
ROSEN ....Fool to Emperor Maximilian I
BERDIC............................*Joculacator* to William the Conqueror
COLQUHOUN ....Jester to the court of Mary Queen of Scots
LONGELY...Jester to Louis XIII
PATCHE................Cardinal Wolsey's Jester, presented to Henry VIII
DA'GONET ....Jester to King Arthur, who later knighted him
PATISON ....Jester to Sir Thomas More
WILL SOMERS...........Court Jester to Henry VIII at Hampton Court
YORICK...................................Jester to the Court of Denmark
AKSAKOFF ....Fool to Czarina Elizabeth of Russia

'Better a witty fool than a foolish wit' — QUINAPALUS

—————————— WILDEAN PARADOXES ——————————

Nowadays, all the married men live like bachelors, and all the bachelors like married men.

I can believe anything provided it is incredible.

It is only the modern that ever becomes old-fashioned.

All women become like their mothers. That is their tragedy. No man does. That's his.

I must decline your invitation owing to a subsequent engagement.

I can resist everything except temptation.

I love acting. It is so much more real than life.

Those whom the Gods love grow young.

The way to get rid of temptation is to yield to it.

He hadn't a single redeeming vice.

Scepticism is the beginning of Faith.

A man cannot be too careful in the choice of his enemies.

There is only one thing in the world worse than being talked about, and that's not being talked about.

A true friend stabs you in the front.

SOME 'SOCIAL' ACRONYMS

FHB	Family Hold Back
NST	Not Safe in Taxis
WHT	Wandering Hands Trouble
PLU	People Like Us
NQOS	Not Quite Our Sort
MIF	Milk In First

4 HORSEMEN OF THE APOCALYPSE

WAR *white horse* · SLAUGHTER *red horse*
FAMINE *black horse* · DEATH *pale horse*

CAFFEINE

Caffeine is perhaps the most widely used psychoactive drug in the world. A basic purine alkaloid, caffeine is readily soluble in hot water, and has a melting point of 235°C. Depending on strength and brew, 150ml of coffee can contain between 30–180mg of caffeine; 360ml of cola contains between 30–60mg.

WAR CRIES OF SOME SCOTTISH CLANS

Clan	*War Cry*
BUCHANAN	*Clar Innis*
CAMERON	*Chlanna nan con thigibh a so 's gheibh sibh feòil* [†]
SUTHERLAND	*Ceann na Drochaide Bige*
MACDONALD OF CLANRANALD	*Dh' aindeòin co theireadh e*
COLQUHOUN	*Cnoc Ealachain*
DOUGLAS FAMILY	*A Douglas! A Douglas!*
MACGREGOR	*Ard Choille*
FARQUHARSON	*Càrn na cuimhne*
MENZIES	*Geal is Dearg a suas*
FERGUSON	*Clannfearghuis gu brath*
FORBES	*Lònach*

† Translates as: *Sons of the hounds come here and get flesh*

——— MRS BEETON'S KITCHEN MAXIMS ———

In *Everyday Cookery*, Isabella Beeton (1837–65) presents her list of culinary maxims. Beeton claims that 'if the novice will commit them to memory, she will have before her the fundamental truths of the art of cookery'.

There is no work like early work.

A good manager looks ahead.

Clear as you go. Muddle makes more muddle.

Not to wash plates and dishes soon after using makes more work.

Spare neither borax nor hot water in washing-up greasy articles.

Dirty saucepans filled with hot water begin to clean themselves.

Wash well a saucepan, but clean a frying-pan with a piece of bread.

Never put the [bone] handles of knives into hot water.

Thrust an oniony knife into the earth to take away the smell.

Search for the insects in greens *before* putting them in to soak.

Green vegetables should be boiled fast with the lid off.

Bread or vegetables left in stock turn it sour.

Roast meat should start in a hot oven.

When pastry comes out of the oven, meat may go in.

Fish boiled should be done slowly, with a little vinegar added.

A spoonful of vinegar will set a poached egg.

Water boils when it gallops, oil when it is still.

A stew boiled, is a stew spoiled.

Melt a teaspoonful of fat in a frying-pan before adding bacon.

Put spare crusts in the oven to grate for breadcrumbs.

Make mint sauce two hours before serving it.

Scum, as it rises in boiling, should be taken off.

No more water than is needed for gravy should be put in the pan.

Salt brings out flavours.

When using ketchup, be sparing with salt.

One egg, beaten well, is worth two not beaten.

Make the tea directly the water boils.

Draw fresh water for the kettle to boil for tea, cocoa, or coffee.

——————— 19TH CENTURY CANVAS SIZES ———————

19th-century portrait painters could purchase canvasses in standard sizes:

Kit-Cat[†]	36" x 29"	Half-Length	50" x 40"
Three-Quarters	30" x 25"	Bishop's Half-Length	56" x 45"

[†] *After the portraits of members of the Whig club which met (c.1700) in the house of Christopher (Kit) Cat. The canvasses had to be cut to fit the rooms' low ceilings.*

——————— AULD LANG SYNE ———————

Should auld acquaintance be forgot,
    And never brought to min'?
Should auld acquaintance be forgot,
    And auld lang syne?

      For auld lang syne, my dear,
      For auld lang syne.
      We'll tak a cup o' kindness yet,
      For auld lang syne.

We twa hae run about the braes,
    And pu'd the gowans fine;
But we've wandered mony a weary foot,
    Sin' auld lang syne.

We twa hae paidled i' the burn,
    Frae morning sun till dine;
But seas between us braid hae roared
    Sin' auld lang syne.

And there's a hand, my trusty fiere,
    And gie's a hand o' thine:
And we'll tak a right guide-willie waught,
    For auld lang syne.

And surely ye'll be your pint-stowp,
    And surely I'll be mine!
And we'll tak a cup o' kindness yet,
    For auld lang syne.

Though usually credited to Robert Burns, it is thought that these lyrics were widely known at the time, and were probably penned by Sir Robert Aytoun.

SPECIFICATIONS

— BOOK —

Paper..................................80gsm vol. 20 Crofton Bookwove
Printing plates......................Eskographics Mondrian Lithosetters
Printing press (text).........................Timson B-format Mini Web
Ink..Cold set black
Printing press (cover)..Komori
Folding & sewing..........................Multiplex Gatherer & Sewer
Trimming..Corona Compact
Marker ribbon.....................................Winters braided 6mm

— TYPESETTING —

Body............*Adobe Garamond*	Dotted tabs....................6pt
Body font size...............8.5pt	Weight of most lines........0.2pt
Baseline grid..............9.51pt	Between title & text.......9.51pt
Title........*Old Style Bold Outline*	Paper-size..........186 x 115mm
Title font size..................8pt	Paper-size ratio.............1:1.61
Small Caps....................85%	Golden ratio...............1:1.61
Copyright page font size......7pt	Bottom margin............20mm
Page numbering..............8pt	Other margins.............15mm

— FONT HISTORY —

Adobe Garamond was drawn by Robert Slimbach, and issued by Adobe Systems Inc. in 1989. The typeface is based upon the original designs and matrices of Claude Garamond (*c.*1490–1561), the legendary French printer, publisher, and designer. Claude Garamond was sceptical about linking roman and italic type, and consequently the italics of *Adobe Garamond* are based on the work of Robert Granjon (*c.*1513–90). Many designers and foundries have issued their own versions of *Garamond*, but Slimbach's Adobe font is perhaps the most elegant, versatile, and visually pleasing.

The designer of *Monotype Old Style Bold Outline*, also issued by Adobe, is not known. However, Old Style fonts are thought to date back to the 1860s, and some credit the work of Alexander Phemister (*c.*1829–94) who was employed at the Edinburgh foundry Miller & Richard. Old Style represented a break from the traditional look of Caslon, tending as it does towards shorter ascenders and descenders, and more elegant, simple serifs.

— MISCELLANEOUS —

Number of mentions of 'Ptarmigan'...................4 (including this)
Tip o' the hat to..Dave Eggers
Preferred British Library reading-room....................Humanities 2
Number of words..37,837
Quantity of beauty required to launch a single ship..........1 Milihelen

———————— VARIATIONS & DISPUTATIONS ————————

The research of this book has shown the actual fluidity of what might be thought hard fact. Below are just a few of the myriad disputes, variations, and possible inaccuracies encountered across the many sources consulted.

[A letter after the page number indicates which of the entries on that page is referred to.]

Corrections or suggestions may be emailed to: comments@miscellanies.info

---------------INDEX---------------

'I proposed to bring a bill into Parliament to deprive

an author who publishes a book without an index of the

privilege of copyright, and, moreover to subject him

for his offence to a pecuniary penalty.'

— LORD JOHN CAMPBELL

------------ A FOR 'ORSES – BOND FILMS ------------

— METRE, DEFINITION – SECOND, DEFINITION —

'There is nothing, Sir, too little for so little a creature as man.

It is by studying little things that we attain the great art of

having as little misery and as much happiness as possible.'

— SAMUEL JOHNSON